new cottage style

Meredith® Books
Des Moines, Iowa

New Cottage Style
Project Manager/Writer: Jean Schissel Norman
Graphic Designer: Brad Ruppert, Studio G
Copy Chief: Terri Fredrickson
Publishing Operations Manager: Karen Schirm
Edit and Design Production Coordinator: Mary Lee Gavin
Editorial Assistants: Kaye Chabot, Kairee Windsor
Marketing Product Managers: Aparna Pande, Isaac Petersen, Gina Rickert, Stephen Rogers, Brent Wiersma, Tyler Woods
Book Production Managers: Pam Kvitne, Marjorie J. Schenkelberg, Rick von Holdt, Mark Weaver
Contributing Copy Editor: Wendy Wetherbee
Contributing Proofreaders: Julie Cahalan, Candy Meier, Nancy Ruhling
Cover Photographer: Jon Jensen
Contributing Photographers: Quentin Bacon, Gordon Beall, John Reed Forsman, Jon Jensen, Bob Mauer, Alise O'Brien
Contributing Photostylists: Bonnie Broten, Sally Mauer, Joetta Moulden, Barbara Mundall, Liz Dougherty Pierce, Mary Anne Thomson
Indexer: Sharon Duffy

Meredith® **Books**
Executive Director, Editorial: Gregory H. Kayko
Executive Director, Design: Matt Strelecki
Senior Editor/Group Manager: Vicki Leigh Ingham
Senior Associate Design Director: Ken Carlson

Publisher and Editor in Chief: James D. Blume
Editorial Director: Linda Raglan Cunningham
Executive Director, Marketing: Jeffrey B. Myers
Executive Director, New Business Development: Todd M. Davis
Executive Director, Sales: Ken Zagor
Director, Operations: George A. Susral
Director, Production: Douglas M. Johnston
Business Director: Jim Leonard

Vice President and General Manager: Douglas J. Guendel

Better Homes and Gardens® **Magazine**
Editor in Chief: Karol DeWulf Nickell
Deputy Editor, Home Design: Oma Blaise Ford

Meredith Publishing Group
President: Jack Griffin
Senior Vice President: Bob Mate

Meredith Corporation
Chairman and Chief Executive Officer: William T. Kerr
President and Chief Operating Officer: Stephen M. Lacy

In Memoriam: E.T. Meredith III (1933-2003)

All of us at Meredith® Books are dedicated to providing you with information and ideas to enhance your home. We welcome your comments and suggestions. Write to us at: Meredith Books, Home Decorating Editorial Department, 1716 Locust St., Des Moines, IA 50309-3023.

If you would like to purchase any of our home decorating and design, cooking, crafts, gardening, or home improvement books, check wherever quality books are sold. Or visit us at: bhgbooks.com

table of contents

introduction - getting started

Any house and every room hold the promise of becoming the cottage you love.
Whether you live in a 1960s ranch, a loft apartment, or a charming bungalow, it's
easier than ever to bring your favorite cottage look home. Use this book as your
personal decorating adviser. You'll find that the newest cottage looks are brighter,
sparer, and more personal than ever before. Learn ways to dress a bed, ideas for
slipcovers, and tips for picking paint colors that suit your cottage sensibilities. What
are you waiting for? Turn the page to get started today.

cottage style today

Cottage style offers more comfort, easier living, and a wider range of decorating options than any other style. No wonder it's an American favorite. It fits at home whether your nest is empty or filled with a family. With few rules of right or wrong, it's easy to adapt your cottage look to suit your changing life. Here's proof that cottage style is perfect for today and tomorrow.

european imports—pages 12-51

Pared down and lightened up, today's cottage with a European accent offers comfort, freshness, and individuality. Gone are the yards and yards of flowery fabrics and the collections that only invite dust. Today's look means saving floral designs for pillows or paintings, editing collections down to a chosen few, and creating light and simple rooms with bare windows and painted woodwork.

american favorites—pages 52-83

The hardworking homes of America's past—farmhouses and bungalows—soften up when introduced to cottage style. Touchable natural-fiber fabrics, painted furniture, personal collections, and soft color palettes reinterpret the style. Original features, such as worn woodwork, wood floors, high ceilings, and great porches, keep the softness from feeling too sweet.

modern updates—pages 84-105

Cottage style might take a modern spin, but it never strays from its classic roots—rooms that embrace human scale, windows that catch views of the garden, and textured materials that meld modern and cottage styles. Look for cottage icons, such as botanical prints, painted furniture, and neutral fabrics, presented in new ways.

today's getaways—pages 106-141

The getaway cottages that sparked the revolution in casual home design offer style for year-round living. Consider how a lakeside cottage can get dressed up for company without feeling stuffy and how a woodsy cottage lined with pine can look hip and young again. It's all in the mix of comfortable furnishings, fun accessories, and favorite collections.

european imports american favorites

modern updates today's getaways

what's your style?

If you're feeling wishy-washy about which cottage look you like best, these questions will help you put your dreams into words and ideas.

There are no wrong answers to this quiz. In fact, you might discover you like a lot of different cottage styles. Many other homeowners do too. That's why you're apt to find seashells in a landlocked farmhouse and Native American prints in a lakeside cottage. So enjoy the questions, think through your answers, and be ready to experiment with your cottage style.

My favorite color scheme for decorating is ...
a. Based on the colors found in a favorite piece of fabric.
b. One main color plus one or two accent colors.
c. Monochromatic with multiple shades of a single hue.
d. Blues, greens, neutrals, and other colors from nature.

If I could hang any chandelier it would be ...
a. One with crystals and beads and lots of detailing.
b. A simple iron shape with curves and scrolls that looks handmade.
c. An oversize round or square lampshade hung like a chandelier.
d. A lantern-look fixture that reflects its oceangoing past.

I love furniture that is ...
a. Inspired by 18th-century design. I'm drawn to the curves and added details.
b. Rustic and hardworking with classic lines. This furniture looks better with wear.
c. Clean-lined and modern. I like simple lines and a spare feeling.
d. Simple with a worn painted finish.

I would decorate my mantel with ...
a. A gilded mirror and a bouquet of white roses.
b. An architectural fragment.

c. Three modern vases or metallic pots.

d. Seashells or twigs in a glass cylinder.

When I walk into a fabric shop, I'm drawn to ...

a. Lush florals and toiles.

b. Classics, such as stripes and checks, in a limited range of colors.

c. Solid-color fabrics with wonderful textures.

d. Durable fabrics, such as denim and ticking.

My most prized collection includes ...

a. Transferware plates, platters, and tureens.

b. Folk art and oddities, such as carved toys, old maps, and concrete urns.

c. Hand-thrown pottery with soft glazes in cream, mocha, and celadon.

d. Nature's objects, such as shells, branches, and pinecones.

My favorite vacation would be ...

a. Traveling in the south of France.

b. Driving on back roads across the United States.

c. Checking out city art museums.

d. Hiking in the mountains or walking on the beach.

My dream house is ...

a. A cottage filled with charming architectural details.

b. A farmhouse with high ceilings and wraparound porches overlooking the garden.

c. A city loft with open spaces and industrial finishes.

d. A casual cottage by the water's edge filled with nature's soothing colors.

MOSTLY A'S: You love the look of European cottages and would be happiest in a place where you can combine your love of collecting with beautiful fabrics and colors.

MOSTLY B'S: Vintage architecture suits you perfectly, whether it's a farmhouse or a bungalow. You're ready to embrace the past and update it for today.

MOSTLY C'S: You're torn between living in a modern loft and loving cottage style. Don't fight it. Cottage ingredients are perfect for softening the hard lines of a contemporary structure. But restrain your cottage outlook to make sure the space feels right for today.

MOSTLY D'S: You've never gotten that favorite vacation getaway out of your mind. Bring the feeling of the lake, sea, or woods home to your house. This livable look offers comfort and ease, the perfect ingredients to make any day seem like a vacation.

CAN'T PICK? Don't worry if you want to pick more than one answer for the questions. It's possible to mix and match and still create a cottage that lives with style. You'll find a lot of examples in the pages that follow.

2

european imports - house tours

American homes inspired by the cottages of Europe pay homage to their English, French, and Scandinavian design roots, but, ultimately, they reflect American sensibilities of comfort, freshness, and individuality. No matter the inspiration, you won't find a pure historical look in the bunch. Solid-color fabrics dominate. Collections, pared down and massed, yield a simpler look than in cottages past. The soft colors and wall murals of Sweden combine with rough woods and bold furniture for a more robust version of the traditional style. If you love the look of these homes, be inspired to create your own version of a European cottage.

french industry

It's no surprise that flea market furniture, painted floors, soft fabrics, and a gentle color scheme can anchor cottage style, but it's surely unexpected that they can make a loft in a former industrial warehouse in New York City look almost like a cottage in France.

A 700-square-foot loft in Tribeca, carved out of the shell of an industrial building, hardly seems the stuff of cottage style. But Liz Dougherty Pierce, a freelance art director and designer, didn't let that deter her from creating a city home that feels as serene and chic as a little cottage in France.

The original beaded-board paneled bathroom, with its European attitude, inspired Liz when she moved into the apartment more than 17 years ago. So did the old tin ceilings and wood floors, and the brick wall along one side. Those elements remain. Liz and her husband, Michael, added the rest to create this soulful city retreat. "When you live in a city as hectic as New York, you need to come home to a place that's visually soothing and peaceful," Liz says. "This loft is like an escape."

Curtain a nook

To create guest sleeping quarters in her small apartment, Liz Dougherty Pierce curtained off a section big enough for a twin bed. "Close the curtains and it feels like you're traveling on a train," she says. All the fabrics feature a simplified version of Indian block prints in one color on an off-white ground. "I think they're the new toile," she says. "You easily can mix all the different patterns."

The reality is that the 9½-foot-wide space needed some visual breathing room, so Liz painted walls, floor, and ceiling a space-expanding shade of soft white. "The best thing I ever did was paint the floor white," she says. "It totally made it feel cottagey." Dove gray and soft blue serve as accent colors in the main room. "When I lived in Paris, I loved the way everything was so gray and felt open, beautiful, and elegant. I just gravitate to that look," she says.

Although her space is small, Liz likes to make a big statement with oversize objects, such as a mannequin and an urn. "I like big things on top of tables. They're such beautiful objects. I like to see them at eye level," she says. When she uses small objects, she unifies them with texture and color to give the effect of one big object. The still life of balls in a stone urn (see page 18) is a perfect example with its gray and silver theme.

Look up for style

In one long room, OPPOSITE, floor-to-ceiling curtains signal the boundary between seating and dining areas. Liz loves to exploit the loft's height. Taking the curtains to the ceiling gives a sweeping effect. "It makes it feel bigger, but it's just trickery," she says. The farm table, painted her favorite shade of soft dove gray, blends with dressier upholstered and slipcovered pieces.

Entertain with a surprise

A still life on the table, ABOVE, shows how Liz plays with the elements of entertaining. She soaks off bottle labels so the wine looks like it has been decanted. "It looks so pretty," she says. Stilton cheese is displayed on its wrapper rather than on a precious plate. This relaxed style is just right for today's cottage.

Some of Liz's tricks are just about making the small space live larger. Curtain panels hang from the 10-foot ceilings and divide the loft into "rooms." Tall screens also define the space. Mirrors reflect mirrors to give the loft more light and "a hall-of-mirrors kind of feeling," Liz says. Furniture in a similar style, "Louis the something," as she describes it, is easy to move about the apartment and regroup in new ways.

A small space might cramp some people's style, but it just focused Liz on what to keep and what to pitch. "It's hard to be a good editor and to really edit your possessions," she says, "but once you start paring down, it feels so good."

Fake the fire

Nothing says cottage as quickly as seating pulled in a circle around the fireplace, OPPOSITE. Who cares that the mantel is real but the fireplace is fake? Liz selected small-scale chairs to fit the small space.

Collect for color

Objects grouped by color create a cohesive look rather than a jumbled mess on a table top, ABOVE.

Accent for drama

Reflect for light and space

Embrace the negative

Group for impact

Accent for drama

A curving wall leads into the only hallway in the apartment. Liz painted the lower half of the wall in a darker shade to accent the curve and provide an easy-care surface that hides wear and tear. She found the old plaster sign part in Sag Harbor, New York. It's just an *objet*, something you would find in French decorating, but it serves to call attention to the curve.

Reflect for light and space

Mirrors appear throughout the apartment because they reflect light and make the small space seem much larger. Liz likes to combine several mirrors on one wall so they reflect the rest of the apartment and create different views as you move through the space. In some areas, mirrors reflect mirrors.

Embrace the negative

An exposed electrical conduit in the studio looks like a style statement with favorite photos and cards tucked behind the metal.

Group for impact

One or two books on a table might not garner any attention. But stack lots of books, especially vintage ones with worn pages, and you create a tabletop worth remembering. Liz bought the French books in Canada.

Drape an alcove

An alcove on one side of the apartment serves as a bedroom. Liz divided it from the rest of the loft with floor-to-ceiling lengths of red and white fabric. The headboard, OPPOSITE, is the original fire door, which is now unused. Shelves fill the space where the door used to slide.

Make room for work

By keeping most of her books in the floor-to-ceiling bookcases, OPPOSITE, Liz maintains a spare feeling in the rest of the loft. An antique desk pairs with a brand-new plastic chair by Philippe Starck called the Louis Ghost chair. It blends with the other Louis chairs but is the most modern version.

Save original details

That's the loft's freight elevator behind the branches, LEFT. Liz changes the scenery, from twigs to a mannequin, BELOW, to suit her mood. The central object, however, always makes a statement.

european with a texas accent

Sink-in furniture covered in slipcovers, floral fabrics, tole trays, toile wallpaper, and vintage linen sheets are the stuff of European cottages—a little bit English and a dab of French. Put them together with country antiques for dressed-up style with a laid-back attitude.

That's the combination Lauren Ross and her husband brought to their circa-1936 Houston home. After buying the house, Lauren resisted suggestions to knock down walls and open the space to match the mega-size new homes nearby. Instead, she kept the original architecture and room sizes intact, saving old windows, mantels, beaded-board ceilings, and cabinetry. As a result, Lauren says, "Every room is small and cozy, and that fits our lifestyle."

Picking the color palette was easy. Lauren admits that pink makes her heart beat a little faster. "Every room in my house has at least a touch of pink," she says. She adds in yellow, blue, and green and uses these colors from room to room.

A mix of wallpapers carries the color themes through the house. Lauren used 10 patterns, most of them mini prints. Wallpaper adds a cozy feeling to small rooms and small spaces,

Mass your collections

A collection of small objects, like this mercury glass, disappears if it's spread throughout a house. Group it in one spot, and it gains impact yet offers a restrained look that's right for today. Use a vintage oil painting or a piece of fabric as a backdrop for the collection.

Build a look on white

Rumpled linen slipcovers snuggle up to bamboo tables in the living room. The solid fabrics and soft colors provide a restful counterpoint to the more colorful parts of the house. A garden table serves as a coffee table and brings the feel of an English garden inside. A round mirror above the mantel simulates a window and adds sparkle. Follow Lauren Ross's lead: She makes sure every room has one chair for comfort and one painted piece of furniture for interest. Keep your home fresh by moving things around, putting some things in temporary storage and bringing others out.

and Lauren even applies it to the backs of bookcases for a surprising touch of color.

Fabrics, too, add layers of color and pattern. Lauren stays away from coordinated fabrics from one line ("too matchy-matchy") and mixes in inexpensive neutrals, such as canvas. Ticking stripes and checks work like neutrals. Antique monogrammed linen sheets and floral fabrics build on Lauren's "collected-over-time" style.

Pretty it is, but this isn't adults-only decorating. Lauren, who has four children under age 10, chooses easy-wash slipcovers, affordable sea-grass rugs, and flea market finds that won't be harmed by the ordinary wear and tear of life with kids. With four males in the house, Lauren knows she can't overdo the frills. In the family room, lots of wood and muted colors keep the space soft but not too feminine.

That spirit of compromise, of making sure everyone is comfortable in a space, is key to the new look of cottage style, even when it is based on the best of European interiors.

Soften with fabrics

Although the look is much simpler than traditional English cottage style, check closely and you'll count seven separate fabrics in the corner of the living room. Mixing and matching fabrics is key to English style. Silk curtains in a colorful stripe dress the windows and provide inspiration for the home's color scheme. White linen covers one chair, while white canvas updates the love seat. Old roses dance across the front of oversize pillows; plaid covers the backs. A French chair wears a new back made from an antique sheet embroidered with a large L. The bench is covered in a soft toile.

Work in style

The same strategies that work in this European-inspired style also make a home work space cozy and charming. For this over-the-garage office, a soft cream paint color brightens every surface, including the floor. Odds and ends of furniture, treated to a new paint job or fresh slipcover, sport a soft neutral or pastel tone. An 8-foot-long table, with a linen skirt that hangs from cup hooks, provides a work surface and storage underneath for baskets and sliding files. More storage fits into the under-eave spaces.

Use restraint

Instead of ruffles and flowers, less-feminine ticking stripes and box pleats add a European feel to the family room. Warm wood tones in a mix of colors, paneling painted white, and drapes in a muted toile keep the palette soft and neutral. Built-in cabinetry provides hideaway storage for electronic gear and shelf space for favorite collections. Lamps add a soft glow that works better than stark overhead lighting. Found objects, such as baskets and vases, become lamp bases.

Add special details

New shelves have a vintage look thanks to softly curved corner brackets. Car siding—8-inch-wide tongue-and-groove wood material—provides a durable wall surface. Ties and ball fringe punctuate pillows.

Soften the kitchen

A slipcovered chair feels right at home snuggled up to the kitchen desk. Curvy legs tie the desk to its French ancestors, but painted bright green, it's perfect for today's style. Rustic baskets look good and work hard. The roll-up shade is made from the same vintage linen as the island cover.

Dress it up

A livable kitchen offers charm and conceals some of the functional details. A washable skirt made from vintage linen sheets covers the island and hides clutter; it's attached using hook-and-loop fastening tape. The island is on casters so it can scoot to one side of the room during parties.

Use restraint   Add special details

Soften the kitchen   Dress it up

Add playful surprises

The adventurous French would love a chest in this eye-popping shade of pink, LEFT.

Combined with flowery tole trays, ABOVE, and needlepoint footstools, it shows how to

make a space feel English, French, and American all at once. Layering—rug on rug, drapes

over blinds, slipcovers over wood chairs—gives a collected-over-time look that's essential

to cottage style. Playful details give hand-me-down chairs new attitude: Rickrack trim

accents edges between wood and fabric, and scalloped hems flirt with straight legs.

Make it pretty

When you're decorating for a little girl who wears pink every day, go all out and make her room as pretty as you please. This color scheme, inspired by the vintage aqua tile in the adjoining bath, mixes pink and white with aqua. Ruffles on the bed skirt and chair slipcovers, flouncy pillows, and soft roll-up shades make the room soft and feminine. For fun details, make pillows from tea towels, cover lampshades with vintage monogrammed sheets so the initials show when the lights are on, and add a sparkly chandelier.

Save the character

The home's original aqua tiles were in good shape and worth saving. Lauren added pink and white wallpaper to complement them and give the bath an up-to-date look. Replacing the door panels in the cabinet at the back of the room with chicken wire over fabric brings the blue of the tiles to the upper part of the wall. A skirt made from an old linen sheet romances the sink. A wicker plant stand keeps folded towels handy.

everyday swedish

Soft grayed colors, elegant furnishings, a tiled stove wall, and rustic decorative painting reflect their 1700s Gustavian roots, but today's Swedish style features a more modern spareness and a warm, casual attitude that suits any house with unfussy architecture.

The Swedish spirit of elegance and austerity perfectly suits homeowner John Maher, who, years ago, fell in love with the rooms shown in Lars and Ursula Sjoberg's book *The Swedish Room.* When he and his wife, Julie Szabo, decided to renovate their small 100-year-old farmhouse in upstate New York, John chose Swedish style. Of course, he didn't want a slavish duplication—and neither did Julie, a fan of ultramodern design.

Their two styles, Swedish and modern, came together when they started working with William Cummings and Bernt Heiberg of Heiberg Cummings Design. This duo combines Gustavian elegance and rustic comfort in their furniture collection and in remodeling projects.

Cummings and Heiberg orchestrated the changes in John and Julie's farmhouse. They changed the living room by adding French doors. They also knocked out the dropped

Gather memories

Found objects displayed on a rustic bench, ABOVE, show how to use collections without destroying the simplicity of Swedish style. A chalky blue painted bench provides a perch for an ever-changing collection of objects.

Focus on hand-painted elements

The shadowy tree mural in the entrance hall, LEFT, repeats themes seen on Swedish walls for generations. The subtle colors and rustic shapes are the handiwork of a Swedish decorative painter. Painting the mural over a rough wall surface preserved the feeling of age that is so important to Swedish cottage design. The mural, however, is softer and more relaxed than those of an earlier era.

Stay flexible

For a small space, furniture that works more than one way offers flexibility. The upholstered chairs in the living room, covered in a mix of leather and ticking, can sit singly or slide together to make a love seat. A stack of cushions works as an ottoman or coffee table. The bold shapes and rustic materials of the seating pieces contrast with typical Gustavian furniture, giving this farmhouse a look that's modern and rustic. The milky tones of the walls and ceiling play against the sheen of the tile behind the wood-burning stove.

ceiling to reveal the original wood structure, installed pine boards on the walls, and tiled behind the wood-burning stove. In the dining room, the new look meant covering the ceiling with pine boards. New wood floors in all the rooms were stained walnut and whitewashed to reflect light. Milk paint in colors from oyster white to marigold prepared the walls for the final flourishes: hand-painted swags, birds, trees, flowers, and words.

With the scene set, John and Julie selected simple pieces of furniture covered in hardworking leather, ticking, and linen. Accessories, too, are reduced to just a few pieces, such as the galvanized tub that holds firewood and the antique wooden folding chairs that serve as art and extra seating. Linen roller shades preserve the view of fields and woods.

It might not be in Sweden, but this American farmhouse speaks a design language inspired by centuries of Scandinavian design.

Make it muted

Milky finishes and soft colors duplicate the look of centuries-old Swedish homes. In the dining room, an exquisite wall painting serves as a backdrop for a dessert table draped with white fabric. Primitive shelves built into a niche create the feeling of a house that has been adapted over time. Chalky whitewashed shelves contrast with shiny handblown glassware based on designs from the 14th to 19th centuries.

Save room for company

A dark wood table that expands to seat 12 anchors the dining room. Chairs and a settee placed around the room draw up to the table when company arrives. Hand-painted swags on the wall and a glass chandelier add elegance to the room. It's the same mixture of rustic chalky surfaces and elegant touches that defined Swedish style in the 1700s. The look now is more spare and less formal.

Accent architecture with color

In the living room, beams overhead were exposed and finished with a coat of oyster white milk paint. To reflect as much light as possible, John and Julie treated the floors to a walnut stain and then whitewashed them. With their blue-gray paint, the new tongue-and-groove wood walls provide a modern interpretation of early wood-paneled walls. The rail system keeps dishware and extra chairs handy for entertaining.

Think rustic

Spare the windows

Mix it up

Warm the hearth

Think rustic

Simple accessories, such as this candlestand, keep the look spare and understated. In early days, candlelight was a necessity, and an untrained woodworker would have made a piece like this to keep or sell. Painting wainscoting is the easiest way to create the look of a Scandinavian farmhouse. In historical Swedish homes, darker colors of gray, red, blue, or yellow were painted on lower walls with a lighter version of the same color on upper walls.

Spare the windows

While some cottage styles might place lots of fabric at the windows, Swedish style keeps them as bare as possible. Here, blown-glass pulleys and leather straps provide the working elements for roller shades made from white linen. The simple shades diffuse sunlight, yet open wide for the view.

Mix it up

Blue and white ticking is traditionally Swedish; leather is a modern twist on the style. The pillows are made from old pieces of tapestry bordered by ticking.

Warm the hearth

Handmade 6×6-inch field tiles pave the wall behind the wood-burning stove, allowing it to sit closer to the wall. The tiled wall provides a safe setting for the hot stove and reinterprets the look of tall, tiled stoves that once heated Swedish homes.

Have a little fun

Treat your collections as sculpture, like this tongue-in-cheek display of irons on a vintage ironing board, RIGHT.

Make your own sunshine

Washing the bedroom walls with marigold milk paint provides a sunny escape even on a gray winter day, OPPOSITE. The tufted headboard is designed to look like an old-fashioned mattress standing on end. A mix of fabrics, including velvet, shows how to expand on traditional Swedish fabric choices.

then and now

	The style	Architecture
	French style in an urban space	**THEN** Urban lofts just weren't the appropriate home for French style two decades ago. **NOW** The painted surfaces, plaster walls, and bare windows of a loft, decorated with a French sensibility, seem closer than ever to a rustic antique house in the countryside.
	Dressy English and French mixed with a casual flair	**THEN** Houses from the first half of the 1900s offered the perfect backdrop for European style, with small spaces and nooks and crannies. **NOW** Cherish an old house and its interesting details. In a new house, add vintage appeal with molding, French doors, hardwood floors, and built-in window seats.
	Gustavian elegance with a modern spareness	**THEN** Pristine interiors with freshly painted floors and woodwork were the backdrop just 10 years ago. **NOW** Any house can become a Swedish cottage. Cover walls with tongue-and-groove wood. Add a Scandinavian-style wood-burning stove with tile behind it. Lay wide-plank wood floors and give them a natural scrubbed finish.

OUR LOVE AFFAIR WITH EUROPEAN STYLE CONTINUES. Every 10 years at least, it's time to consider how a new combination of fabrics and colors can help this age-old style feel fashionably chic. For today's look, edit your collections to replace clutter with simplicity. Sort through your possessions to create rooms that tie to the past but live in the present.

Backgrounds	Fabrics	Collections
THEN Warm yellows and reds offered a colorful palette for the Provence look. **NOW** There's more to France than Provence. A restrained palette of gray, soft blue, and off-white creates a soothing retreat that draws on the colors of Paris and makes a small space live large.	**THEN** Toile remained the fabric of choice for centuries. **NOW** Indiennes fabrics, printed with one color plus white, show how even a classic pattern can be simplified for today's sparer look. Gone are the multiple patterns with many bright colors.	**THEN** One-of-a-kind objects filled every surface in French homes. **NOW** One-of-a-kind objects still define French style, but the look is more restrained, with one or two objects on a tabletop. Unexpected collections honor the French tradition of living with unusual pieces.
THEN In the 1980s, paint colors and wallpaper patterns on the walls made the background as busy as the rest of the room. **NOW** Paint large rooms in soft tones to create simple backgrounds. Use wallpaper sparingly—in the backs of bookshelves, in small rooms, or in kitchens with plain white cabinetry.	**THEN** A dominant large-scale floral established the mood 15 years ago. Supporting fabrics came from a matching collection. **NOW** Cover sofas and large chairs with solid-color slipcovers. Save large florals for pillows. Try floral draperies in a room with painted walls. Mix it up. Don't buy all your fabrics from the same company or designer.	**THEN** Clutter was key to the look, with a wide range of collections covering every wall and tabletop. The look started to change 10 years ago. **NOW** The style honors the idea of less is more. Collections grouped with restraint seem more important and more relaxed. Objects stored away can rotate by season.
THEN Too-sweet blue and white anchored this look 10 years ago. **NOW** Use soft grayed colors, such as chalky blues and greens, to keep the Swedish mood. Add in rustic colors, such as rust and oatmeal. Whitewash over natural woods. To bring in additional color, consider a modern interpretation of a mural.	**THEN** Small-scale geometric prints in blue and white, filmy window sheers, embroidered table runners, and ruffles were the '90s interpretation of Swedish style. **NOW** Step away from the too-soft look with hardworking leather, handsome ticking, and linen. Use casual textured fabrics on formal furniture. Add soft linen panels at the windows.	**THEN** Everything was out on display. Open cupboards, mantels, tabletops, and plate racks were filled to the brim. **NOW** Simplify. Put clutter away. Consider placing only one collection that's used regularly in an open cupboard. Unexpected surfaces, such as a bench, fill in for traditional display pieces.

3

american favorites - house tours

As early settlers moved from the coasts to the heartland, the architectural landscape changed. The homes of the early 1800s gave way to bungalows and farmhouses, familiar house shapes that remain popular today. Each offers the opportunity for creating a cottage look that stays true to its architectural and decorating traditions but offers easier and more comfortable living for today's families. Dressed up a bit and softened with cottage style, the houses in this chapter showcase why these American favorites endure.

southern charmer

Tucked high in the Blue Ridge Mountains, this Southern cottage dates from the late 1800s. Now lovingly restored, its softly aged walls, painted floors, and livable porches reflect its heritage; its spare furnishings and simple color scheme make it right for today.

Built as a summer cottage, Carol Faust's year-round home was once part of a community built by wealthy planters in the South. Neglected for years, the little house had fallen on hard times. "The day I first saw the cottage, we turned down an overgrown lane, drove through the cool shade below tall Southern pines, eased past the flowering rhododendrons, and there it was—dreary and forlorn," she says. The real estate agent had warned Carol that the house was in bad condition. None of his other clients would even get out of the car to take a closer look.

It was love at first sight for Carol. It's not that she romanced away the problems—broken windows, rooms smelling of mildew, and vegetation that shut out sunshine. It's just that she could see the potential in the cottage's high ceilings, tall windows with old wavy glass, four fireplaces, and four sets of French doors opening onto wide porches. "I loved the fact that everything in this 1,500-square-foot house was original," she says.

Carol, with the help of a contractor, plunged in to heal the little house. Once the major updates were out of the way, she tackled the rest of the work on her own. "Little by little, room by room, I have gently restored my beloved cottage, transforming it into a bright, airy year-round home without destroying its historic patina," she says.

Furnishing the house was a matter of instinct for Carol. She filled the rooms with finds

Save the patina

In a vintage cottage, it's best to preserve any original finishes that suit your scheme. Carol Faust loved the look of her home's original plaster walls, complete with layers of peeling paint. She gave the walls a hard scrubbing to remove loose paint but otherwise left them as she found them. Simple objects, such as glass jars, wicker-covered bottles, and ironstone, add character without jarring the palette.

from the flea market and a mix of collections, from ironstone and white pottery to apothecary jars and shells. Carol started her shell collection in childhood. "Now the house has a quirky beach-house-in-the-mountains kind of style," she says.

Preferring a relaxed look, Carol has created a home that looks like it has evolved over time. Most of the furniture is light and airy—reed, rattan, and bamboo. "I don't suppose I've paid more than $10,000 for the entire contents of my house," she says. She uses touches of brown to ground the color scheme and highlights of blue for one simple reason. "Blue feeds my soul," she says.

The final effect is spare and serene. "Simplicity suits this house," she says, "and it suits me too."

Merge the line

French doors join the living room to the porch. Rattan furniture, painted white and softened with ticking-covered cushions, brings the feeling of the porch indoors. Collections in white stand atop a wood cabinet that once held nuts and bolts in a hardware store.

Paint wood floors

To give her cottage a bright look, Carol painted all the wood floors, except the kitchen's, a glossy white. Gloss paint reflects more light than flat paint and offers easy care as well. The walls and woodwork wear white, a look that's clean and fresh. Carol added a coatrack to the hallway that stretches from one porch to another.

Add a surprise

Vintage office furniture might seem too businesslike for a cottage, but the contrast between metal and reed creates a delightful surprise, RIGHT. Carol often spots old office furniture at flea markets.

Save a family piece

Carol snagged this early kitchen cupboard, OPPOSITE LEFT, from her father's basement, where it had languished for decades. She had new doors made, painted them white, and filled the cupboard with her favorite things.

Romance the kitchen

Carol found the cast-iron, enameled double sink, OPPOSITE RIGHT, resting in a rusty metal cabinet when she bought the house. She traded a piece of furniture to have someone build a new cabinet for the sink. The beaded-board door panels add the perfect cottage detail.

Sleep in sunshine

Carol's bedroom, LEFT, gathers light from morning to night. She filled the space with her collection of shells, alabaster, coral, and crystals. Plain bed linens in shades of white add to the serenity, proof of the power of neutrals to strike a romantic note.

Build a collection

Carol's favorite grouping of shells, BELOW, shows how their variegated colors and textures warm up this all-white room. The shells were a serendipitous find thanks to a classified ad in the local newspaper. It read: "Shell collection. Free." "My car was loaded with shells by 8 a.m.," Carol says.

Dress the beds

In the guest bedroom, RIGHT, 1940s twin metal beds are layered with nostalgic blue and white striped summer spreads from the same decade. The dark woods and blue stripes provide a cottage feel in the otherwise all-white space.

Add drama with photography

Carol mounted the vintage black-and-white photographs of palm trees in flea market frames and set them on the guest room's fireplace mantel, BELOW. The Mission oak chair is a $5 find from a Saturday morning church sale.

Arrange seating on the porch

Carol uses some of her collection of reed furniture on the porch, OPPOSITE. The white floors flow from inside onto the porches. A hammock in one corner provides a breezy spot for a summer nap.

Build an outdoor living space

Carol started laying brick in her yard, BELOW, to eliminate a mud puddle that appeared by her back door after every rain. She liked the look so much, she just kept adding bricks, building a patio that suits cottage style. Many of the flowers she loves most—hollyhocks, irises, tulips, lily of the valley, violets, and delphiniums—were already in the yard, lying dormant in the shade. "Once I took down some trees to let in the sun, they came back to life," she says.

farmhouse fresh

A New England antiques dealer shows how easy it is to soften the no-nonsense attitude of a farmhouse with cottagey slipcovers, curtains made from antique floral panels, walls the color of butter and blueberries, and collections ranging from ironstone to iron beds.

A dinner invitation might seem an unlikely way to start house-hunting, but that's exactly how Jocie Sinauer and David Chicane discovered their farmhouse. One problem: It wasn't for sale. Six months later when the century-old house went on the market, they snapped it up. "It was just the kind of place we'd dreamed about," Jocie says. "Not fancy, just a simple farmhouse."

Updated by its previous owners, the house was ready to be moved into. "David had the Pottery Barn armoire," Jocie says. "I brought everything else." That meant collections of everything. "David's more of a minimalist," she says. "I'm the exact opposite. I've always been a collector."

Jocie started collecting as a little girl and now sells an eclectic mix of antiques at her shop, Red Chair, in Peterborough, New Hampshire. She favors old-fashioned pieces that fit a cottage setting—iron bedsteads, antique quilts, white ironstone, and painted

Pick a bouquet

Hydrangeas in an ironstone pitcher and yellow roses on curtain panels instantly say cottage, OPPOSITE. Combining the flowers with stripes and solids gives them a fresher look than layers of floral patterns. Jocie Sinauer found the garden table and matching chairs at an auction and updated the cushions with antique ticking.

Revamp porch furniture

Fabrics such as matelassé on the sofa, RIGHT, provide cottage patterns in a solid color. This neutral palette works outdoors because it puts flowers growing in the garden on display.

furniture, all pieces that have found their way to her home. "Anything too grand wouldn't work in these small rooms," she says.

The result is a home that feels as fresh as just-cut daisies. Beds are layered in old linens and piled high with antique pillows. Sun pours in through windows curtained with vintage fabrics. Old mirrors are hung to reflect the light. Vintage light fixtures cast a soft glow.

Jocie's favorite room? The back porch, of course. It stretches the length of the house. At night, she and David sit on the rattan settee and count the stars. By day, they breakfast on the porch, seated around a white glass-top table. Lengths of antique flower-filled fabric soften the sun's glow.

"When we moved into this house, all my furniture fit just perfectly," Jocie says. "I decided that was a good omen. It's as if we were always meant to live here."

Relax the dining room

A casual table and chairs keep the dining room, OPPOSITE, from feeling too formal. Jocie stores some of her collection of ironstone in the antique cupboard. A schoolhouse light fixture provides a warm glow.

Give in to comfort

An oversize sofa overflowing with pillows anchors the seating area, ABOVE. Slipcovered in linen, it matches the fabric on the ottoman, which also functions as a coffee table. Sink-in seating and a put-up-your-feet ottoman offer a new kind of cottage comfort. To keep clutter at bay, Jocie hid electronic gear in the armoire.

Find a new spot for display

A trio of ironstone pitchers occupies the windowsill, RIGHT. It's fun to play with your collections, moving them to special spots as the seasons change. The lidded casserole dishes leave the kitchen for this stairway landing, where they hold odds and ends. "I love the simple lines [of ironstone]. It matches every pattern, even fine china. Is there anywhere in the house you can't use it?" Jocie asks.

Store with style

A dresser and wicker baskets keep bathroom gear handy but out of sight, OPPOSITE. The worn finish on vintage pieces, including the dresser, grounds the cottage look and adds character. An old Dutch towel, once used in a laundry for wringing out excess water, now does duty as a bath mat.

Make it blue

The guest room walls sport a soft shade of cornflower blue, OPPOSITE. Jocie used the color as a backdrop for white linens and a flowery quilt. "A beautiful fabric adds a splash of drama to a room, especially when you're working in whites," she says. She found the iron headboard at a local auction; the oval mirror cost $5 at a flea market. Many of the elements of cottage style are still very affordable.

Savor the small things

Jocie started out collecting buttons, LEFT, and they're still one of her loves. She likes to keep some of them on display in small dishes. Clustering small objects in containers is one way to keep clutter under control. Consider large glass cylinders for everything from shells to ocean-polished rocks.

a better-than-new cottage

After years of "improvements," a vintage 1940s cottage steps back to its beginnings thanks to a sensitive remodeling that brought a vintage fireplace, pedestal-base tub, and pretty paint colors home for good. Outfitted with paint-scrubbed tables, hooked rugs, and a slipcovered sofa, this bungalow looks at once old-fashioned and up-to-date.

Interior designer Michelle Riviera, of Boulder, Colorado, says she didn't realize how difficult it would be to reinvent a 1940s house after it had been subjected to many remodelings over the years. "The woods aren't the same, the skilled labor force isn't what it used to be, and they don't make molding profiles like that anymore," she says.

Her litany of concerns aside, Riviera not only improved her client's home, she managed to bestow it with a gracefulness that it had never known. Part of that grace came from turning a mountain-view cottage into one that would look equally at home on an oceanfront lot. To do that, Riviera added porches with columns, an abundance of French doors, and a white picket fence. Inside, the theme continues with built-in

Go for neutrals

Selecting fabrics, paints, and furnishings from a neutral palette keeps the overall effect from feeling too girly, OPPOSITE. Simple matchstick blinds and a carefully edited selection of collections maintain a spare, unfussy feeling. The fireplace mantel and built-in cabinets are new to this house. Michelle Riviera, ABOVE, searched a local salvage yard to find pieces of the proper scale.

Replace cabinets with a pantry

To help a small kitchen work big, storage is organized in a pantry behind French doors, OPPOSITE. That eliminates the need for space-grabbing upper cabinets. "I put a 1-foot space in front of the interior shelving so you'd see the reflection of the glass rather than the items behind it," Riviera says. Beaded-board cabinets, wood floors, and a German-import refrigerator add charm.

Embrace the era

Vintage pieces, such as the farm table and 1950s green vinyl chairs, ABOVE, look perfectly at home in this 1940s cottage. The glass fixture also dates from the era. Riviera recommends research to get things right. "Don't be overly attached to your own vision of the past. It may not be accurate," she says.

bookcases and cabinets, beaded-board paneling, and a pastel palette of creamy yellow, pale periwinkle, and mint.

Before the paint could be applied, however, every room needed to be transformed. Riviera created a focal-point wall for the living room with an antique fireplace surround and built-in bookcases she found at a local salvage yard. "When it comes to making old things fit in a new room, you really need a builder and carpenter who are game," she says.

In the small kitchen, which Riviera describes as a 3-foot walk-through to the basement, she created a pantry behind French doors so she could eliminate some overhead cabinets. A built-in bench and bookcases streamline the eating area while providing storage and display space. The net effect is a kitchen that works hard in the skimpiest of space.

A 1970s second-floor addition had to stay, but Riviera turned it into a light-filled master bedroom and bath with views to the mountains. "The main objective was to make a good-size master suite on the front of the house to capture the great views," she says. Now, the space looks like a finished attic, just the effect Riviera wanted for this vintage bungalow.

The real lesson? Being old-fashioned is perfectly right for today when you live in a reformed 1940s cottage.

Spare the details

To create a simple master suite, Riviera kept things spare and serene with periwinkle walls and a minimum of furnishings, OPPOSITE. The French doors open onto a second-floor porch. Authentic glass doorknobs were installed on this and most doors throughout the house.

Open up to the view

An old dresser with a been-out-on-the-porch paint job and antique glass drawer pulls nestles into a corner of the master bedroom, RIGHT. The porthole window is a nod to the seaside feeling the homeowner wanted.

Don't let the good ones get away

When you find something that speaks the language of cottage, buy it even if you have to store it for awhile. The green medical supply cabinet, **OPPOSITE LEFT**, was discovered "as is" for $5 on a junking mission. Now, it fills a storage need and makes a style statement. Automotive paint can restore a worn metal piece like this.

Salvage for style

To create this wonderful nostalgic bathroom, **OPPOSITE RIGHT**, Riviera traipsed through salvage yards and flea markets to find pieces such as the pedestal sink and bathtub. Even the sconces and wall cabinet are vintage pieces. Bringing them back home adds nostalgia to the bathroom.

Bathe in luxury

A pedestal-base soaking tub, **LEFT**, might have been strictly utilitarian at one time. Today it's the sweetest of cottage luxuries. Romance the look with hexagonal tile and beaded-board paneling, all in white.

then and now

The style	Architecture
 Southern cottage in a gently preserved state	**THEN** Houses built as Southern retreats in the 1900s had elegant built-ins and woodwork. Time and part-time occupants took their toll. **NOW** Preserving a cottage's gentle state of decay offers a style that's more rustic and casual than intended when the home was built.
Aired-out New England farmhouse	**THEN** Up to 1950, boxy rooms with little architectural detail dominated farmhouses. **NOW** In houses with rooms of ample size, few alterations are needed. Preserve and honor basic moldings and architectural details. Open up small rooms by removing walls. Adapt a small bedroom for use as a bathroom.
Bungalow reborn	**THEN** Over time, additions and remodelings hid the simple charms of 1930s and '40s bungalows. **NOW** Built-in bookcases, beaded-board paneling, porches with columns, and an abundance of French doors—either replaced or updated—create a cottage look that's old-fashioned and up-to-date.

YOU PROBABLY FELL FOR THE HOUSE—an American farmhouse or a '30s bungalow. Now you're wondering how to help it bridge the eras from then to now. That's easy. Leave fancy fabrics and finishes behind. This look calls for a spare touch, restrained palette, and handsome furniture. Your goal is to honor the workmanlike attitude of these house styles.

Backgrounds	Furniture	Collections
THEN Dressy wallpaper, waxed wood floors, and deep colors set the mood until 30 years ago. **NOW** Original plaster walls with cracks and peeling paint honor the home's origins. Glossy white paint on the floors fills the house with light. White paint on woodwork creates a simple background.	**THEN** Upholstered furniture and wood tables and chests provided comfort in a getaway house. **NOW** Reed, rattan, and bamboo furniture, all painted white, provides a beach-house atmosphere that's relaxed and at home in the mountains. Simple cushions covered in vintage linen or ticking keep the mood casual and unfussy.	**THEN** The finery of the era found its way to summer getaways for wealthy Southerners. **NOW** Natural objects give this cottage style a casual spin. Found objects, such as shells from the beach and just-picked ferns from the woods, mix with wicker bottles and ironstone for a collected look that's soft and serene.
THEN Scrubbable painted walls, all in one off-white color, made farmhouses easy to maintain. **NOW** Paint covers the walls, but the color palette is more personal, softer, and varied than in the past. That's why you'll find walls painted in pretty colors rather than just white. Wood floors topped with rugs still anchor rooms with a warm tone.	**THEN** Furniture served a purpose, such as a table for food preparation or a cupboard for storing fresh preserves. **NOW** An eclectic collection of furniture works well in plain farmhouse rooms. Curves and curlicues add surprising contrast. Look for fancy chairs to mix with farm tables. Place a Victorian parlor chair next to a modern sofa.	**THEN** Objects, such as bowls and mirrors, served a purpose. **NOW** That attitude of utility prevails in collections that look good and work hard. Bowls and platters sit on open shelves above the kitchen countertops, where they can be appreciated as well as used. Watering cans might grace porch steps.
THEN Remodeling often left old houses with all the charm of a brand-new builder house. **NOW** Returning the charm means creating focal points, such as fireplaces and bookcases, picking a color palette to romance the look, and limiting the number of materials. Coherent design makes it all flow.	**THEN** Overstuffed and heavy, dark furniture filled the spaces so they no longer felt comfortable. **NOW** Furniture from the era—1930s and '40s—helps establish the mood, but with restraint. Too many old pieces can make a house feel like a museum. Add in new pieces, especially comfortable upholstered chairs and sofas that are the right scale for small rooms.	**THEN** A vintage cottage might look busy, with a lot of flowery fabrics and collections in a rainbow of colors. **NOW** Take a tip from designers who create a focal point from one large piece, such as a vintage cupboard, or from a collection, such as cream-color McCoy flowerpots. Simplify to make the pieces you love stand out.

4

modern updates - house tours

Modern and cottage hardly seem like words that go together. But they're the perfect pairing to describe what's happening to cottage style today. Just think of what defines a cottage space: rooms that feel cozy, windows to the garden, furniture that's people-friendly, and accessories drawn from the spirit of collecting. On the pages that follow, those elements are present in two homes that reach back to the past and forge into the future. Take a look. This simple, modern version of cottage style might just be how you're wanting to live.

85

modern comforts

A new house proves that it's possible to create a livable urban cottage within a contemporary framework. Although this home appears modern on the surface, a closer inspection reveals classic cottage elements: a connection to nature, comfortable rooms, and touchable textures.

Tom and Mary Anne Thomson were looking for a different kind of house when they decided to sell their 1910 home in St. Louis and build on the lot they owned next door. "We looked closely at ourselves, at how we want to live, at what inspires us, and at what our bodies and souls need to return to balance," Mary Anne says.

Although their search for serenity and comfort led them only feet from the house where they raised their children, their design journey took them much further. Their new home—a modern and spare cottage—rests comfortably in a neighborhood filled with brick houses noted for their classic center-hall floor plans and open front porches.

Tom, an architect, designed the house to be compatible with its historical neighbors. That meant merging past and present. The new house features brick cladding, a

Mix new and old

The entry sunroom, OPPOSITE, is a modern interpretation of a front porch. A replica of a Gerrit Rietveld chair, built by a friend 35 years ago, takes pride of place in the light-filled room. A white-painted bench contrasts with the lines, colors, and texture of the chair. It's the perfect pairing for Mary Anne and Tom Thomson who love contemporary elements mixed with older pieces.

Draw up to the hearth

Casual furniture gathers around the fireplace in the living room, LEFT. The asymmetrical slate hearth replaces the mantel as a display space. The Thomsons perch their collection of handmade birds throughout the space.

Repeat patterns

With their gridded pattern, shoji screens duplicate the look of traditional French doors, BELOW. The sliding screens separate the sunroom entry from the living room.

symmetrical façade with French doors, front porches, and a sloping roof—design elements that seem ageless and modern. Interior spaces arranged in a C around a courtyard offer glimpses of the garden and fulfill Mary Anne's wish to be faced with nature at every turn. In fact, many rooms offer views of the front yard and the courtyard.

The interior look Mary Anne and Tom orchestrated flows naturally from the architectural design. Rooms are simply furnished with clean-lined pieces. Many of the windows are unadorned, leaving views of the garden unobstructed. A variety of materials—wood, stone, and sisal—enhance the connection to nature. Even the artwork—branches on the living room hearth and leaf prints on the bedroom wall—blurs the indoor-outdoor line.

The elements of cottage style are interpreted in a more modern way in this new house, but look closely and you will see the cottage within. "It's a home with a simpler, no-frills style," Mary Anne says. "Something more resides in designing with less. More beauty, less bravado."

Be bold with modern elements

The open kitchen, **RIGHT**, has a more modern edge than most of the rooms, thanks to the material choices: stainless steel, glass, and stone. Frosted-glass shelves take the place of traditional glass-paned cabinets.

Plan for indoor and outdoor dining

With its long table, stone floors, and French doors leading to the courtyard, the casual eating space, **OPPOSITE**, is known as the "Tuscany room." A second set of French doors opposite these turns this into a screened dining pavilion. "This is our room for feasts in the countryside," Tom says.

Create visual warmth

Soft fabrics, a centered fireplace, and windows overlooking the garden pull from the roots of cottage style, OPPOSITE. The bed and love seat are drawn closer to the hearth for visual warmth. The muted green wall reflects the color of the trees visible through windows on both sides of the room.

Draw on nature

Large-scale botanical prints, LEFT, mimic antique botanical-book page prints that appear in many classic cottage rooms. Flowers in glass cylinders, rather than curvy vases, reflect a modern attitude.

Soften with texture

The texture of Native American baskets, LEFT, plays against smooth wood, nubby upholstery, and plush carpet to soften the modern cottage.

Make ordinary special

Every object and texture matters when you edit furnishings down to a chosen few. A bowl of soaps, BELOW, wrapped in rice paper, clearly showcases the beauty of common items.

Create your own spa

A limited palette of colors and materials adds serenity to the master bathroom, OPPOSITE. The windows face east, so the morning sun pours in. "The treetops give a sense of being in the air," Mary Anne says.

thoroughly modern cottage

Tidy cottage-size rooms might seem unlikely raw materials for modern style, but this little Oregon bungalow reveals how bright colors, spare furnishings, and updated cottage icons can yield a look that's hip, hot, and still so comfortable.

The familiar adage about good things in small packages neatly describes the 1,000-square-foot bungalow Erin and Michael Weis call home. As an interior designer, Erin often designs interiors for houses with over-size rooms, huge windows, and high ceilings. But don't think she's disappointed that her own house is on the small side. "A small house gives you this kind of comfort level when you walk in. You're not overwhelmed with the space," she says.

That doesn't mean that just any small house will do. Erin bought her little paradise because it had a fireplace at the end of the living room that could be a focal point, a floor plan that allowed foot traffic to flow easily, hardwood floors underfoot, large doorways between spaces, and rooms in need of some updating. "You can find a good house and turn it into something wonderful," she says.

The work started with a cosmetic redo of the brown tile fireplace and didn't stop until Erin had created a style she describes as traditional with a modern flair. Big, bold botanical prints framed and matted in white add graphic punch to an apple-green wall. That green, in fact, is Erin's favorite color. Paired with crisp white and an occasional third color, such as orange, it's a fresh, young update of a traditional cottage color scheme. "The more colors you add, the busier it gets," Erin says, noting that palette restraint is key to her look.

Dine with color

A jolt of apple green brightens the dining room. White woodwork, curtains, and furniture provide contrast. Keeping the palette simple—shades of green plus white—is Erin Weis's favorite way to update cottage style and make a small space feel larger.

The furniture has a modern edge, with its straight rather than curvy lines. Fabrics in bold two-color prints transform classic furniture into modern pieces. But these chairs and sofas all offer sink-in seating, a key element of cottage style. Each piece of furniture has plenty of breathing room around it, a practiced restraint that lets this little cottage live big.

Erin has a few tricks she guarantees will give a small house a lot more style. For instance, you'll find a space-expanding mirror in every room. "Adding a mirror is like adding a window. It's another view into the room," she says. "I love the way mirrors catch light and bounce it back into a room."

Erin also uses paint colors that make spaces appear larger. "When you add a dark color to the room, it makes the space shrink," she says. Muddy colors also visually reduce space. Window treatments should be simple, too. "Don't cover up your windows," she says, unless privacy is an issue.

That's smart advice for a look that's perfectly modern, perfectly cottage.

Scale down

A demilune table and chairs with open or no arms furnish one side of the living room. "Pay attention to scale," Erin says. A small cottage like hers looks better if the furniture is proportional to the size of the rooms. That doesn't mean all the pieces have to be small, but a massive sofa, for example, can overpower.

Add personality with botanicals

Vintage botanical prints, enlarged and printed on pure-white paper, look totally modern matted and framed in white. Grouping them creates one large piece of art. It might take several copies to get the background white, Erin explains, but you'll find that all the colors become brighter during the copying process.

Create a fireplace focal point

Make a space seem larger by turning a fireplace at one end into the focal point, OPPOSITE. That requires a makeover for most 60-year-old fireplaces, like Erin's. Adapt her idea: Paint the fireplace white, add white tile around the opening, and top the mantel with a space-expanding mirror for an instant improvement.

Keep it simple

Newly made in classic cottage style, milk pitchers filled with matching blooms offer new-cottage style, RIGHT. It's just the pop of color Erin loves to use in her cottage. This restraint—one style of container and one type of bloom—gives a vintage cottage modern appeal.

Make it relaxing

White expands; cool colors, such as green, recede and calm. What could make for a more relaxing feeling in a tiny bedroom? Erin added a few tablespoons of apple-green paint to white paint to give the walls the look of lime sorbet. She dressed the bed in a green quilt. "You come in and just want to take a deep breath and relax," she says.

Revamp a vintage piece

A new coat of chalky milk paint turns a cabinet into a charming dresser, **LEFT**. To give an aged effect, the paint was applied using a dry-brush technique. A mirror looks like a window over the dresser.

Create a soft spot

Extra details, such as a pile of pretty pillows, **BELOW**, make even the smallest bedroom feel luxurious. They're also a smart way to continue the green and white color scheme. "You just want to jump in the bed and lie down with all those pillows," Erin says.

then and now

Modern home with a cottage soul

THEN Sleek metals and glass gave modern houses an uncomfortable edge in the 1980s.
NOW Rustic wood, tumbled stones, and French doors bring a livable quality to modern houses. Doors and windows connect a house to nature and draw in sunlight that embraces its occupants. Shoji screens and level changes, rather than walls, divide rooms.

Vintage bungalow with a new attitude

THEN Cottages built in the 1940s featured small rooms and simple finishes.
NOW To bring this look up-to-date, accent architectural details with white paint. Use mirrors as "windows" to open up small rooms. Simplify to create clean lines, for instance, by eliminating natural brick around a fireplace.

A FEW BRAVE SOULS ARE REINTERPRETING COTTAGE STYLE into a look that's modern yet familiar. Thanks to livable rooms, spare furnishings, and fresh palettes, the look we've loved for generations grows even more creative when graced with modern ideas. The good news is that this style—called cottage-modern—works as well in a new house as in a vintage one.

Backgrounds	Fabrics	Collections
THEN White walls, light wood finishes, and metal accents provided a cool look. **NOW** The views of gardens through windows and doors create the best of backgrounds. Woods with a natural finish and rustic quality warm up the surfaces. Paint with a touch of blue or soft green offers a softer palette than stark white.	**THEN** Leather in dark tones offered the cleanest interpretation of the modern look in the '90s. **NOW** Texture provides interest when fabrics lack pattern. Fabrics include worn leather, old linen, and nubby cotton. Throws in touchable textures soften seating, which is covered by solid fabrics with a soft hand, helping relax contemporary shapes.	**THEN** A few clean-lined objects in modern materials became needed focal points. **NOW** Organic objects, such as carved birds, birch branches, stone bowls, and rustic benches, ground the design. Make a statement by placing a few pieces of a collection on a piece of furniture built for display. Furniture itself serves as a collection when arranged so pieces look sculptural.
THEN Rose beige was all the rage in the '40s, acting almost like today's neutral. **NOW** Try an eye-popping hue, such as apple green or tangerine. Use just one color in various shades throughout the house, even adding just a tablespoon or two of colored paint to tint white paint. Keep windows as bare as privacy allows.	**THEN** Bold flowery prints in a palette of blue, green, pink, and yellow covered furniture and windows in the 1940s. **NOW** Solid-color fabrics with texture are the backbone of this look and let the color of paint and accent fabrics pop. Bold-pattern fabric in white plus one color updates the look of vintage florals.	**THEN** Collections of small objects in a wide range of colors filled every surface. **NOW** Bold displays, such as reprinted botanicals framed to create one large work of art, are one way to update favorite collections from the '40s. Objects in multiples and with modern silhouettes also help define the look.

5

today's getaways - house tours

The new cottage style we love—relaxed, comfortable, and personal—traces its origins to little houses built as getaways. The carefree lifestyle they promised continues to be a way of living many of us want today. It's still within reach. Knotty-pine walls might serve as a backdrop for contemporary art in a woodsy retreat. Colorful florals can make a lakeside house pretty and livable. Walls in ocean blue suit a house by the sea. But even if you don't own a house by water or woods, you'll want to live as though you do. The three houses featured here show why.

living by the lake

White wood walls and rows of windows can transform even the darkest, dingiest lakeside cabin into a cottage perfect for today's carefree living. Here's how one homeowner used layers of colors and collections to dress up her little house without losing its laid-back attitude.

By the time Bonnie Broten returned to her home state, she had bought, redone, and sold many houses, big and small. But her heart still longed for one perfect place. "I always thought, 'What if I could wave a magic wand? What kind of house would I live in?' My answer was always the same: a little cottage on a Minnesota lake," Bonnie says. She found the perfect one just minutes from Minneapolis.

On closing day, the 1,200-square-foot cottage with tiny windows, claustrophobic rooms, and dark walls—some knotty pine and others dark green paint—hardly looked the stuff of lifetime wishes. But just look at it now. Bonnie spent four months turning it into her dream home. New windows stretch the length of the porch out back facing the lake. French doors open the front of the house to a sheltered deck. A new bath nestles into a space near the back door. Skylights scoop in daylight.

While remodeling opened up the rooms, the least expensive change, a coat of white paint, made a dramatic difference. The paint turned knotty-pine car siding into the perfect cottage background for Bonnie's collection of white slipcovered seating, floral paintings, patterned pillows, and eclectic fabrics.

Although many of the pieces in Bonnie's house have been with her for years, her return to Minnesota influenced her decorating style. "When I got here, I started adding lots of color, deep colors such as cranberry red and hot pink," she says.

Plan for change

To keep a cottage look fresh without spending a fortune, rework what you have. Bonnie Broten slipcovered these chairs in white; underneath they're upholstered in a black and white check. Lengths of fabric layered over the table give it one look now and a fresh look with a change of fabrics. Neutral blinds at the windows suit all the fabric options and add a warm, natural touch.

"Those colors counter all the white snow out the window almost half the year." The colors appear on everything from chairs to collections. The backdrops remain neutral—white painted walls and ceilings in all but the bedroom and natural hardwood floors. They provide a less-fussy version of cottage style.

Bonnie's ability to mix things up—combining toile with faux leopard, putting one fabric on the front of a chair and another on the back, and stacking English baskets with African ones—freshens a cottage style that's a perennial favorite. "I suppose it looks like fancy furniture in a cabin, but it's really a little cottage that looks dressed up but comfortable," Bonnie says.

Gather round the fire

A fireplace lends a cozy feeling to any cottage, especially when surrounded by comfortable chairs, OPPOSITE. The trick to using a lot of chairs in a tiny space is to select small upholstered pieces. In summertime, minimize the fireplace by drawing the chairs in to partially hide the fireplace opening.

Set the scene with collections

Use the mantel as a gathering spot for your collections, ABOVE. It's a fun way to "organize" favorite objects and add color. "I decided the easiest way to bring flowers into the house was to buy paintings," Bonnie says. Dark oil paintings become graphic rather than sweet when hung on pure-white walls.

Pick see-through furniture

A glass-top table is a perfect solution for a small dining area, RIGHT. It offers function without visually filling space in today's less cluttered cottage schemes. A glass table also can air out a traditional cottage dining room that usually features a wood table.

Treasure overhead space

In a small cottage, the space overhead can be just as important as the square footage, OPPOSITE LEFT. To keep this area light and bright, Bonnie painted the ceiling white, added a new loft railing, and installed skylights. The space overhead gives this cute little cottage a more modern edge. The living area and dining area are one space, a strategy that visually expands both.

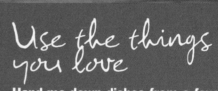

Use the things you love

Hand-me-down dishes from a favorite grandmother add color to the dining room sideboard, **ABOVE**. To give the arrangement more impact, Bonnie cut roses so they create a tight ball just above the vase's rim.

Plan for traffic

Give chairs personality

Take comfort outside

Pamper the kitchen

Plan for traffic

French doors and interior doorways keep traffic flowing in a circle through Bonnie's cottage, from the living room, through the kitchen and porch, and back again. That's a great way to make any small house live large. Editing collections also helps. "I used to have a wall full of tole trays. Now I have one," Bonnie says of the area above her dining room sideboard.

Give chairs personality

Chairs are worth the expense of re-covering if you can buy them affordably. "I'll come dragging out [of an estate sale] with some chair no one else would want," Bonnie says. She then uses several fabrics for a one-of-a-kind look. Because the back of a chair only requires a small amount of fabric, Bonnie might buy a yard or less of antique toile on eBay or, in the case of this striped back, use a new dish towel.

Take comfort outside

A deck overlooking the lake is prime real estate on summer afternoons. For cottage appeal, plump the chaise longues with striped cushions and snuggle colorful pots of flowers up to the deck railing. An outdoor spot is crucial to cottage style whether it's a deck, dock, patio, or porch.

Pamper the kitchen

In the tiny galley kitchen, Bonnie reworked cabinets, painted them white, and added butcher-block countertops. New terra-cotta tiles are 12-inch squares, a size that makes the space feel larger. Bonnie couldn't match the tile color to the wood floors, so she opted for a color that blends. Recessed lighting works best with the kitchen's low ceilings.

Scale down furniture

A small cottage has to make room for people. The trick is to select small-scale pieces, such as the love seat and chairs in the television area on the porch, RIGHT. An upholstered ottoman provides put-up-your-feet comfort. Bonnie chose small-scale furniture for all the seating areas in the house.

Divide and conquer

When you deal with an irregular room shape, as in this enclosed porch, BELOW, divide the space into separate sitting areas. Because the room is 36 feet long and only 9 feet wide, Bonnie angled the love seat to provide access to the desk behind it. The bookcases that flank the French doors are new but built to match the kitchen cabinetry. Such consistency of design is crucial to creating today's cottage style in a small house.

Turn a small room into a jewel box

A tiny bedroom with barely room for making the bed becomes pretty, not cluttered, with a mix of patterns in a palette of black and white, LEFT. "The wallpaper actually makes the room seem bigger," Bonnie says. Use wallpaper dramatically in just one room for the most impact.

Add design spunk to pillows

Needlepoint pieces and vintage flower prints might look too predictable. That's why Bonnie pairs these old familiars with a feminine fringe or a welt or boxing of faux leopard, BELOW. "I like to perk them up a bit," she says. The backs of the pillows feature fashionable contrasting prints.

back to the woods

After serving one family for 50 years, a 1950s ranch owes its latest transformation to its lakeside location. A grandson revamped the much-loved house into a warm cottage with kick-off-your-shoes comfort, hardworking fabrics, and wood-paneled walls.

The 1950s ranch house that David Grenell's grandfather built by the water didn't have the appropriate woodsy attitude, but that was nothing a little remodeling couldn't fix. After all, David knows his way around home improvement projects. His job as a project manager for David L. Smith, Ltd., a Chicago design firm, involves just about every phase of remodeling and redecorating.

The project in his own home was the talk of the office. After much thought and a lot of input from his colleagues, David reconfigured the walls to create a new kitchen, double-sided fireplace, raised seating area, and defined entry. The new walls were treated with tongue-and-groove knotty pine boards. The finish is soft rather than shiny, a fresh take on this cottage style. The other walls in the house now feature paint or a vinyl wall covering that looks like grass cloth.

Introduce a little glamour

Glass and metal dress up the living room, OPPOSITE, but a variety of textures keeps the space grounded to its lakeside location. David Grenell loves to collect natural objects, such as the driftwood hung on the wall, and pair them with elegant pieces, such as the sunburst mirror. New striped fabric on the bamboo furniture, ABOVE, offers a modern interpretation of classic ticking.

Improve the view

Removing the top half of the kitchen wall improves the cook's view and provides space for an eating counter, OPPOSITE. A mirror creates the illusion of an interior window, a simple way to visually expand space in a small house.

Freshen up

A sofa adds a touch of comfort to the dining room, BELOW. Leather chairs, aged to perfection, surround a gateleg table. Mixing eras and styles freshens any cottage.

Add interest with texture

A small house might not be able to handle too many colors or pieces of furniture, but texture is always welcome, RIGHT. David mixes soft velvet fabrics, crisp sea-grass rugs, metal upholstery studs, and worn leather chairs.

By coordinating backgrounds and repeating elements from space to space, David ensured that rooms would blend seamlessly.

With the remodeling finished, David set to work furnishing the house. The pieces arrived from "anywhere and everywhere," he says. He re-covered his parents '70s sofas with dark green chenille. That same fabric shows up on wicker and wing chairs, and even a window seat. Wooden blinds and sea-grass rugs add texture.

David's collection of natural objects appears throughout the house, hung on the walls and set on tabletops and bookshelves. He gathers items while working on various projects around the country: Rocks came from Colorado, driftwood from the San Juan Islands, and shells from Florida.

Although updated cottage style flatters the little ranch, what's most important is what has always been key to David's family. "The house is loved and lived in," he says.

Paint for impact

Brown walls create a handsome backdrop for David's collection of artwork, ABOVE. He describes the color as a "really deep brownish green. It's really soothing." An eclectic collection of artwork and antiques includes a 1950s headboard and nightstand, purchased by David's grandfather when he built the house.

Collect from one era

Enhance a collection's style by displaying it on a compatible piece, such as this mid-century modern cabinet, OPPOSITE. David started building his collection when he was 16.

Divide for livability

A fireplace covered in knotty pine separates living areas and marks the original exterior wall of the house. In rooms that feel too large to be comfortable, dividing space with a fireplace or large piece of furniture can create the cozy areas essential to a cottage look.

Put anything on a pedestal

David placed this 1930s light on a pedestal to make it the center of attention. The German light is called a mesmerizer. It wasn't for sale when David first spotted it, but he kept returning to the store until the owners finally sold it to him. Three chains suspend the globe in front of a concave mirrored plate. Heat from the original gas lamp turned the fixture's blades so the globe would rotate.

Make a scene

Turn the objects you love into a dresser-top tableau. These pieces reflect David's collecting passions: paintings, sculpture, and pottery. Because he doesn't cram things together, each piece can be admired.

Try symmetry

Symmetry often gives interiors a restful attitude. Matching plates and chairs balance the pine cabinet. David replaced clear glass door panels with panes of ribbed glass to disguise the contents of the cabinet, which he uses as a bar.

Divide for livability

Put anything on a pedestal

Make a scene

Try symmetry

seashell cottage

Undaunted by new construction, one homeowner proves that when it comes to creating cottage style, it's what's inside that counts. Here's how she built cozy spaces into an open floor plan, added age with flea market finds, and crafted an elegant look that's relaxed enough for the beach.

The perfect little cottage doesn't always exist, especially in that just-right location. But that didn't phase Deborah Whitfield. She turned a brand-new 1,800-square-foot duplex at the beach—fresh from construction and featuring one large living space—into a charming getaway cottage to share with her husband, Robert Nash.

Deciding on a style for the beach house was easy. "I knew I didn't want fishy-fishy," Deborah says. For years, she had kept a magazine page that showed an old shell mirror, probably from the 1800s. "I was smitten," she says. An avid collector of Victorian shell assemblages, Deborah had amassed quite a collection in more than 20 years of sifting for shells at flea markets.

Now, the shells play a starring role in her beach cottage. Favorites gather in a pine bookcase, sit on top of shelves, and fill glass containers to overflowing. Deborah made the mirror that hangs in the dining area, and she now makes and sells shell mirrors.

The shells even set the cottage's color scheme of cream, white, and muted blue, except in one bedroom that's painted an eye-popping shade of turquoise. "The longer I lived in the house, the more I wanted a color that would reflect the water around me," Deborah says. "Sometimes you have to live with a house to know what you want."

Making a house livable, however, is something Deborah does with ease. Worn

Dress up for dining

Even a beach cottage can make room for fine dining. The tabletop, made from boards salvaged from a tobacco barn, sits on new legs aged with black paint. Slipcovers give the chairs a dressy look but also offer easy care. Deborah Whitfield made the mirror by attaching shells to plywood, using construction adhesive and wire.

Plan for pets and people

A beach cottage is apt to be filled with visitors. That's why Deborah chose comfortable upholstered pieces to anchor the living room, OPPOSITE. The coffee table, with its worn finish, invites sandy feet.

Shelve a collection

A Victorian Era organ top, repaired and repainted, creates a focal point as a shelf over the sofa, ABOVE. Deborah fills the shelves with local shells and statues of her beloved egrets. "They're like little metal soldiers," she says.

furnishings with a cottage attitude suit her style. "My family can come here and put their feet on the coffee table, and I won't fret," she explains. "Things are worn already so they're easy to live with." The coffee table, in fact, is a marriage of a top from one table and a base from another. Total cost? $20.

After scouring junk shops for great buys, Deborah treats them to some TLC. She refurbishes some for her business, Cottage Nest Antiques. Others find their way home. Deborah fixed a worn lamp for the dining room with plastic wood filler and coated it with a thin layer of what she calls "shabby plaster." A shiny brass chandelier sports a new coat of black paint to match the bedroom. New wheels turn a wood cabinet into a movable island.

This easy-care interior leaves time for what's really important at the beach: kayaking to Egret Island to watch her favorite shorebirds in action, sharing a meal with friends who own the other half of the duplex, and boating on those blue waters of the Atlantic Ocean.

Fill a cupboard

After collecting shells for more than 20 years, Deborah found an old pine bookcase to house her favorites, RIGHT. "This cabinet will stay for the life of the cottage," she says. Robert installed an antique newel to give their new staircase vintage character.

Reflect your location

A cottage by the shore is the perfect place to showcase items with a seaside attitude. Vintage letters spell "sea" on one wall of the living room, BELOW. The circa-1805 painting features a woman harvesting clams on the shoal. Even the brass-tipped oar is a vintage find.

Use cabinet tops as display shelves

Wicker-wrapped bottles create a still life on top of the kitchen cabinets, OPPOSITE. When your kitchen is part of a great-room, treat it just as you would the adjoining area. Deborah added wheels to a wood cabinet to create a movable island that adds warmth to the airy all-white space.

Keep loved objects within view

A kitchen windowsill filled with favorites provides a view for the cook. The vintage basket, LEFT, shells included, cost Deborah just 50 cents.

Display in glass

A collection of beautiful small pieces makes a statement when stored in clear glass containers, RIGHT. Deborah loves to substitute mirrors for the old prints she often finds in vintage frames.

Adapt a chair

Affordable and interesting, chairs can be used for more than seating, ABOVE. Deborah bought this French chair for $5.

Revamp and restyle

A Victorian Era bed painted black shows one way to update a vintage piece. Deborah found the bed parts in two states for about $200 and put them together. She also painted the brass chandelier black and treated the lamp base to a "shabby plaster" finish.

Embrace the outdoors

What could be better than a porch with a great water view and a shady spot to catch the breeze? This favorite outdoor space, OPPOSITE, functions as an indoor room with soft seating and a scrubbed-top table.

Find a new use

Deborah's favorite clamshell is large enough to serve as a bowl, ABOVE. Taking the objects you love and giving them new purpose perfectly suits the cottage life.

then and now

	The style	Architecture
	Lake living with a dressed-up attitude	**THEN** Small rooms with unfinished or wood walls, tiny windows, and open porches suited part-time living 30 years ago. **NOW** Tear down walls to open up small rooms to make airy spaces that stretch to vaulted ceilings. Replace one window with a wall of windows to the view.
	A '50s ranch with kick-off-your-shoes comfort	**THEN** Built in the 1950s and added on to through the years, the basic ranch treasured utility over beauty. **NOW** Revamp the floor plan to create open living areas. Integrate the kitchen to keep the cooks in the thick of things. Retain a fireplace to divide seating areas and add warmth.
	A new house by the sea	**THEN** Original coastal cottages built in the early 1900s suffered from small rooms and odd floor plans. **NOW** New beach houses stretch up for the views and include plenty of windows and doors. Fewer walls ensure large open spaces that adapt when company arrives. Vintage architectural pieces build character into the new spaces.

IN THE 1970S AND '80S, A TRIP TO THE SHORE, lake, or woods meant sacrificing style for a no-fuss way of living. Today, you can create a living-easy space without leaving style at the door. Easy-care slipcovers, hardworking wood finishes, and touchable textures mean that any getaway can get dressed up for play.

Backgrounds	Fabrics	Collections
THEN Dark and woodsy, cottages featured knotty-pine walls and a palette of dark earth tones. **NOW** A light palette often provides the most dramatic change. Knotty-pine paneling used today features a natural matte finish rather than yellow varnish.	**THEN** Utilitarian fabrics in dark tweeds and plaids offered the best defense against sand and wet bathing suits in the 1970s. **NOW** Washable canvas slipcovers offer a tough surface; gathers soften the look. Pretty florals and graphic checks, new and vintage, look at home in today's dressier lakeside retreats.	**THEN** Duck decoys and fishing poles in the corner were more for use than show, even 15 years ago. **NOW** Pretty objects gathered over a lifetime give a cottage year-round appeal. Place vintage dishware and colorful bowls where they're pretty to look at and handy for everyday use. Collect old furniture and give it a fresh coat of paint.
THEN Basic painted walls and simple trim defined a ranch house 50 years ago. **NOW** A double-sided fireplace clad in wood complements wood paneling used elsewhere to give a house a warm, cozy feel. Other textures, such as grass-cloth wall coverings and sea-grass rugs, supplement the wood walls.	**THEN** Straightforward fabrics were durable but light on looks and touchability. **NOW** The new look is all about texture in elegant fabrics such as velvet and linen. Leather, trimmed with brass studs, refines the look even further. Every fabric is chosen because it looks even better as it ages.	**THEN** New objects of the era, from pottery to paintings, were put on display. **NOW** Pottery from the 1940s and '50s is still popular, but display is more important. That might mean carefully editing the collection and finding a perfect furniture piece on which to display it. Gather favorite objects and use them as wall art, to serve a meal, or as a lamp base.
THEN Seaside cottages were as rustic as those along lakes. Every surface reflected the need for easy care and durability. **NOW** Create spaces that live for a weekend or year-round. Use paint to reflect the colors of sand and surf. Finishes on wood flooring make it last even in a seaside location.	**THEN** Furniture covered in vinyl and plastic shades at the windows were short on style and long on durability **NOW** More durable fabrics make it easier to find great style you can live with inside or out. Solid-color fabrics that can be washed, or bleached if needed, add style. Ticking stripes in cotton add accents of color.	**THEN** These temporary quarters featured a ragtag collection of objects. **NOW** The beach is the perfect place to showcase a collection of shells. But don't expect an unsophisticated approach. Shells look elegant in glass containers and on shell mirrors. Vintage light fixtures, updated with paint, offer a collection that works hard.

6

room by room-living spaces

Somewhere in the evolution of the American home, families deserted the formal

spaces at the front of the house. It's not surprising. The informal family room and

eating area near the kitchen offered easier living, put-up-your-feet comfort, and cozy

charm. So what's happening today? Families are once again returning to those front

rooms, but the look is all about comfort. Washable slipcovers, painted finishes, simple

shapes, and a restrained palette allow people to live with style and ease. The

transformation is celebrated here with rooms, such as the one, *right,* that show how to

pair a new relaxed attitude with classic cottage elements.

living spaces

Inviting the spirit of the cottage into your home means taking the "do not enter" sign off what were once formal rooms. Here are 10 things you can do to create living spaces that are truly live-in spaces.

1. Provide comfortable seating mixed with tables, ottomans, and lighting, so you can sit and read for an afternoon or invite friends to linger after dinner.

2. Group furniture around a focal point, such as a window, fireplace, or artwork, to organize a space and create a view.

3. Mix dressy with casual. Dress down formal furniture with painted finishes and washable fabrics.

4. Edit to keep rooms light and airy. This includes colors and patterns as well as furniture. Space is good.

5. Make room for your treasures, but don't keep everything out at once.

6. Add a pretty detail. It could be a scallop on the edge of a slipcover or a floral pillow.

7. Leave windows bare or barely covered with simple blinds and curtain panels.

8. Add flowers and leaves, real or on fabrics, dishware, and wallpapers.

9. Make rooms feel bigger by choosing paints and fabrics in similar hues.

10. Use texture—nubby, woolly, or rough—to soften the formality of fancy fabrics and make cottage style more livable.

Build your own cozy nook

Go for contrast

Spread the sparkle

Build your own cozy nook

Built-in bookcases settle down to the business of making a house feel like home. By leaving space for a banquette, there's also a place to hang a treasured pair of photographs. Solid-color throws add a punch of color that's only temporary, a great strategy for anyone who loves to change colors with the seasons.

Spread the sparkle

Mirrors do much more than reproduce the view. They transfer the sparkle of sunlight to all corners of the room. In a small living space, expand the view and the light with a mirror that stretches from floor to ceiling. If you place it behind an airy piece of furniture, the mirror frame almost disappears.

Go for contrast

A modern settee combined with vintage farm and French furniture looks thoroughly modern yet decidedly unexpected against a backdrop of rustic stone. Such a surprising mix is one way to infuse cottage freshness into a room.

Pick your pattern

Fabric treatments turn any window into a focal point and establish a color scheme. Pair the pattern with solid-color fabrics in a complementary hue. If you need to cover a window for privacy or sun control, simple blinds or shades with curtain panels provide the freshest look.

Pick your pattern

Pare down for comfort

A palette of white-on-white for walls, woodwork, window shutters, and furniture ensures simplicity in a cottage by the sea, **RIGHT**. Texture in the form of sisal rugs, wicker bottles, and pressed botanicals keeps the look interesting. The drop-leaf table was cut down to serve as a coffee table.

Collect by color

In the sunroom of the same home, **BELOW**, a favorite china cabinet wears its original paint—white outside and sage green within. It's a soothing backdrop for a collection of white ironstone. Gathering collections in a spare palette creates harmony. A tiny white picket fence above the window serves as a charming valance.

Dress for dinner

It's not only guests who should arrive dressed up for dinner. Slipcovers give standard dining room chairs a softer attitude. This fitted top says elegant while the gathered skirt says cottage. It's a fitting partnership for breakfast, lunch, and dinner.

Introduce modern elements

This little living room has all the basics of cottage style: white slipcovers on soft upholstered pieces, floral pillows, filmy window coverings, and vases of flowers. But don't expect this to look like a cottage from 20 years ago. Elements such as the Philippe Starck floor lamps and the metal and glass coffee table ensure a cottage that's modern at heart.

Add a color surprise

In this dining room, yellow walls provide a background for a collection of blue and white transferware dishes. Walls paneled to within a few feet of the beamed ceiling and painted white add cottage flavor. Nothing works as hard as white paint to visually expand a dining room that measures just 12×13 feet.

Put your table to work

The condition of the table doesn't matter when you skirt it to the floor with hardworking cotton canvas. In a small house, this trick makes room for storage as well. If the table is set only when company comes, turn it into a library table for day-to-day use.

Dress for dinner Introduce modern elements

Add a color surprise Put your table to work

Match scale

When your house offers up a small dining room, keep it charming with a table and chairs perfectly matched in scale, ABOVE. You might be limited to serving buffet meals to a crowd, but you'll find many ways to use your table for two. Upholstered chairs let you linger after dinner.

Bring the garden indoors

Who says a garden table and chairs can't take up permanent residence inside? This vintage set, RIGHT, looks relaxed and inviting in a small dining room. French faience and its English equivalent, ironstone, match the soft off-white set.

FABRIC

Material differences

Here's how to use fabrics in your cottage.

● **Pick your colors.** Select fabrics first, then match paint colors to your choices. For a no-fail scheme, use two patterns in the same colors.

● **Vary the scale.** Consider a large-scale pattern to set the palette, then support it with a cast of solids, checks, and stripes. Test them in rooms by draping them over the sofa or bed, or from curtain rods.

● **Use vintage materials.** Trims, yardage, bed linens, lace, and table linens offer the basics for gently aging a room.

● **Add a flower or two.** Cottage interiors often reflect the gardens outdoors, so include some florals in the mix.

● **Lavish on the yards.** For bed coverings or slipcovers, go for full gathers and deep pleats. They'll feel much more luxurious. Use fabric to relax formal chairs and to cover up a worn sofa or table.

● **Splurge and save.** Use affordable fabrics when you need a lot of yardage for window treatments or sofa slipcovers. Splurge on expensive fabrics to use in small doses on a chair or pillow.

● **Play with details.** Add ties to slipcovers, edge curtains with gathered trim, or cover buttons to use on pillows.

7

room by room—relaxing spaces

Getaway cottages introduced all of us to a relaxed style of living. It's no accident that bedrooms
and bathrooms, those most personal of spaces, are where cottage style really works
its easy-living magic. It makes perfect sense to pair luxurious details with the intimate sizes of
bedrooms and bathrooms to create snug retreats. The look is easy to achieve. For a bedroom,
mix feather-filled pillows and comforters, soft colors, and sentimental accessories, *opposite*.
Turn any bath into a spa with a claw-foot tub, pedestal sink, and pretty light fixtures.
It's the simplest way to stage a getaway each and every day.

153

relaxing spaces

Comfort is personal, and nowhere more so than in the bedroom and bathroom. Here are 10 ideas to help you choose elements that will relax you.

1. Make the bed the focal point. Dress it simply with beautiful linens in a collection of solid neutrals or make it classic cottage with a floral pattern in pastel shades.

2. Create a dressing area. It might be as simple as a vanity table in a corner of the bedroom or as elaborate as an entire room devoted to primping and dressing.

3. Add details that matter. Consider trim along the edge of a lampshade, the perfect doorknob for a closet, or a decorative pull on a window shade.

4. Soften the windows. Privacy counts, of course, so dress your windows in layers. That might include shades or shutters that close, plus curtain panels for color and luxury.

5. Provide a showcase for a collection. A dresser top or built-in bookcase offers display space. Use silver bowls and ironstone washbasins to hold jewelry, scarves, or spare change. Vintage linens, hung in layers over the footboard or on a towel rack, play up cottage style.

6. Install pretty light fixtures in the bedroom

Accent with red

Accent with red

Red and white checks and toiles keep a pink cottage-style bedroom from feeling too feminine. Quilted white fabric slipcovers the headboard, an inexpensive way to make a big change.

Double the style

Twin beds dressed in vintage quilts snuggle under the eaves of a guest-room alcove, a charming and comfortable retreat for overnight visitors. The worn finish on the bed frames is perfectly at home with the worn quilts on the beds and vintage fabric glued onto the bedside table.

Create a cocoon

A pretty tulle canopy hangs from the ceiling in this tiny bedroom, enclosing the bed without dividing the small room. Toile, stained with tea, becomes a charming slipcover over a modern leather chair. The look is both modern and cottage-fresh.

Create a cocoon

Double the style

Create a bed of flowers

A combination of floral patterns, all in shades of pink, dresses up a guest bedroom, RIGHT. A neutral background makes the bed the star. Feminine touches, such as the lace on the slipper chair and ruffled edging on the lampshade, contrast with handsome sisal carpet and a pine plank ceiling.

Sacrifice for beauty

To create a bathroom as beautiful as this, OPPOSITE, you'll probably have to sacrifice a bedroom. It's worth it if you can create an elegant space for bathing. Wood walls, floors, and ceilings keep the room from feeling too sweet. Vintage hooked rugs blend with the blue-gray floor.

and bath. Chandeliers are finding favor. Consider sconces too, new or old.

7. Tone down new mirrors. Frame mirror glass in vintage plaster frames for a soft look. To create a worn look, rub metallic paint over the frame's surface, then rub off most of the paint with a soft rag.

8. Layer for luxury. Combine quilts and dust ruffles on the bed, soft rugs over carpeting, and tablecloths and lace squares on bedside tables. The fabrics also offer inspiration for a color palette.

9. Choose vintage bathroom fixtures. Claw-foot tubs, pedestal sinks, and wood medicine cabinets add cottage charm to any bath. Look for new or antique.

10. Pick a color scheme that soothes and relaxes. This is your getaway space, so keep the palette soft and muted.

Fool the eye   Build with character

Fool the eye

It might look like a log-walled bathroom, but this effect is achieved with wallpaper. A claw-foot tub shows its versatility, looking as comfortable here as it would in a more feminine bathroom.

Build with character

A brand-new bathroom has an old-fashioned look thanks to beaded-board paneling. The tongue-and-groove boards stretch across the ceiling and up the walls. Windows on three sides create a sunlit tub alcove.

Make that a double

Side-by-side pedestal sinks offer double the style and double the function. Classic features, such as beaded-board paneling and mirrored vanity cabinets, can transform any bathroom into one with cottage style.

Incorporate industry

Hardworking industrial pieces, such as this office swivel chair and 1920s medical cabinet, enhance a cottage bathroom. Antique liquid measuring jars from a French apothecary hold makeup brushes.

Make that a double Incorporate industry

COLOR *Picking the palette*

There's a rainbow of color in every decorating store. Here's how to make the best choices for your cottage.

⊙ Take your room's visual temperature. Use blues and greens to cool down a sunny, southern-facing room, pinks and reds to warm up a sunless, north-facing room.

⊙ Try a no-fail monochromatic scheme with a bold color, such as sunshine yellow for the wall paint and a soft color, such as putty, for the sofa upholstery. Add white trim and furnishings to sharpen the contrast.

⊙ Mix three or more neighboring hues from the color wheel for an analogous scheme. Pick colors of the same intensity—the brightness or dullness of a color—so each hue carries equal weight.

⊙ Play with space. Warm hues, such as yellows, "advance" and make a space feel cozier. Cool colors, such as blues, "recede" and make a room feel bigger. Combine warm and cool colors to intensify their temperatures.

⊙ Work with light. As sunlight changes and is replaced by artificial light, wall color changes too. Gray, taupe, lilac, and celadon are prone to color shifts. Plan well and you'll love your paint color day and night.

⊙ Let color set the mood. Energize a child's bedroom with light, bright hues, and calm a bathroom with soft neutrals. To change your mood by season, add fresh color with pillows, glassware, and paintings.

⊙ Try favorite hues in a new proportion—for instance, blue walls and white furniture instead of the opposite.

8

room by room-kitchen spaces

The kitchen is already the hub of the home. Why not make it the hub of cottage comfort? Whichever version of cottage style suits you best, you'll find it easily transforms a kitchen, such as this one *right*. The changes are simple. Pretty colors, painted cabinets, and soft fabrics give kitchens visual comfort. Hardworking surfaces and well-planned work areas offer comfortable working conditions. That sense of ease translates into a room that smoothly adapts from party central to short-order restaurant.

kitchen spaces

The kitchen may be the hardest-working room in the house, but who wants to be reminded of that when it's time to sit down and relax with a cup of tea? Here are 10 ingredients that will make you forget about cooking, at least for the moment.

1. Preserve cottage basics. Wonderful old tile, charming cabinets, or a vintage sink might be the cornerstone of a kitchen redo. If they're already in your kitchen, they'll start your remodeling on the right track.

2. Update the cabinets. A coat of paint can easily transform any tired kitchen. If the cabinet finish is good, just replace the knobs to give the doors a facelift.

3. Add shelves to hold everyday gear and collections. Consider removing a few cabinet doors and painting the interiors to show off dishes and cookbooks. Or, remove upper cabinetry along one wall and replace it with shelves. The trick is to edit your collections so the shelves don't become too full.

4. Install a wood or tile floor. Hardwood flooring finished with polyurethane is easy to maintain. A floor of ceramic tile also offers fresh footing.

5. Hide recessed lighting and task lighting. Let the effect of the light show rather than these basic lighting fixtures.

6. Supplement task lighting with a handsome hanging fixture. Install it where it will have the most impact, perhaps over the kitchen table or island.

Warm up

A corner fireplace adds a cheery note to the kitchen, OPPOSITE TOP. With an island nearby, it's easy to work or eat within view of the fire.

Uncover assets

Storage stretches up to use every inch of a low ceiling, ABOVE LEFT. Because the cabinets are light and the floors neutral, the dark-beamed ceiling garners its due attention. Shiny surfaces, such as the granite countertop, spread light around.

Go for the diagonal

Stretching tiles on the diagonal can make a narrow galley kitchen look wider, OPPOSITE BOTTOM. Oversize tiles stretch space more than small tiles. Use two colors of tile to create a checkerboard, a common cottage pattern.

Customize for character

Details, such as the beaded edge on the cabinet panels and the sculpted edge of the countertop, give this cottage kitchen, LEFT, extra style. Open shelves instead of bulky cabinets let you see from countertop to ceiling.

Freshen a cabinet

Here's a quick, budget-smart makeover: Remove recessed cabinet panels and replace them with chicken wire and fabric, stapled in place. This countertop looks like ceramic tile, but it's really self-adhesive, vinyl-coated paper.

Make your move

Turn almost any piece of furniture into a movable kitchen island by attaching casters. If the top is too small for your needs, screw a larger one in place.

Build for storage

A pantry adjacent to the kitchen is the prettiest way to increase storage without clutter. Lower cabinets keep most gear under wraps. Dinnerware and antiques fill the upper shelves.

Add furniture details

Chunky legs secured in the toe-kick area give these new cabinets a furniture look. Shelves above the counter enhance the effect of a vintage freestanding cupboard. Study vintage furniture pieces for elements you can use to soften a kitchen.

Freshen a cabinet

Make your move

MEMORABILIA

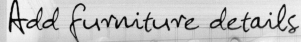

Add furniture details

Build for storage

7. Turn a closet into a pantry to store everything from packaged food to a collection of vintage dishes.

8. Eliminate clutter. Make space for appliances in cupboards rather than on countertops, keep cooking gear in drawers, and put staples, such as flour and sugar, in simple glass canisters.

9. Provide comfortable seating. Soft cushions on benches and chairs invite guests to linger. Add an upholstered chair and a small side table if you have the room.

10. Make room for a vintage piece of storage furniture, whether it's a white painted cupboard or a wall cabinet edged with twigs.

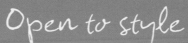

Open to style

Although an open kitchen might be new to cottage style, it's a surefire way to bring a casual attitude to the space. Cabinets bend around a corner to hide some of the utilitarian appliances, LEFT. A wood-topped island looks like a sideboard rather than a kitchen working surface. The color scheme of the kitchen provides a neutral background for the berry and white fabric in the family room, BELOW.

Stretch above the eaves

Use what you collect

Simplify for impact

Opt for vintage details

Stretch above the eaves

A small kitchen feels much bigger after a remodeling project reveals the slope of the roof. A triangular window keeps the ceiling light. Cabinets in basic white pair with yellow, green, and a touch of red for a lively color scheme.

Use what you collect

Collections for the kitchen often have a utilitarian aspect. After all, they're on display but ready for use every day. That's the beauty of open shelves. They offer handy storage and make a design statement.

Simplify for impact

In this tiny kitchen, stainless-steel countertops and modern-style metal chairs add a clean-lined look to quintessentially cottage beaded-board cupboard doors and a turned-leg country table. The cabinets hanging above the counter feature doors made from antique window screens.

Opt for vintage details

Green glass pulls and knobs look perfectly in tune with the 1930s. They're a colorful way to make a new kitchen feel at home in a vintage house. Collections in the same hues reinforce the color favorite.

BACKGROUNDS

Setting the scene

Walls, floors, and windows set the cottage mood. Here's how to get them right for today.

WALLS

○ Dress walls with wood. Place it vertically, stretch it 5 feet high for a wainscot, or vary the plank width for a new take on tradition. Try a matte finish for an updated look.

○ Paint using this year's palette for an inexpensive update. Stencil an allover pattern rather than a border.

○ Use wallpaper as an accent. Add a bold pattern to a small room. Apply a small amount of paper in the back of a bookcase or on a dresser.

FLOORS

○ Try wood floors. Paint old floors for a fresh look. Install maple rather than oak.

○ Create colorful patterns. Lay ceramic or vinyl tiles in fun colors but classic patterns.

○ Bring the outside in by duplicating the wood or stone floor from the porch or patio.

WINDOWS

○ Sparely dress windows. Use a roll-up shade for privacy. Add self-stick films for sun control.

○ Connect to the garden with French doors.

○ Practice restraint. Keep curtains tailored and simple, such as panels shirred on a rod.

9

room by room-outdoor spaces

The natural connection between a cottage and garden is celebrated with outdoor "rooms" created within the sheltering arms of giant trees, porches outfitted with sofas and rugs, *right.* and dinner parties held outdoors. Now you're as apt to hang a chandelier from an outdoor trellis as from a ceiling indoors. Vintage cupboards appear on the porch, filled with collections. This outdoor expansion "grows" living space as well, a boon to cottage life. New all-weather fabrics handle moisture, sun, and humidity with ease. Life on the porch has never been so sweet.

171

outdoor spaces

The line between indoors and outdoors is more blurred than ever, thanks to a renewed interest in the garden. Here are 10 ways to "decorate" your yard.

1. Build "rooms" in the garden using plants as architecture, letting their shapes form walls and ceilings. The sense of enclosure makes outdoor spaces feel cozy.

2. Plant with a color scheme in mind. If you're using blue and white in paint and fabrics, choose flower colors to complement.

3. Plan a focal point for every space. It might be a view down a row of trees or an urn that looks perfect from a nearby bench.

4. Create seating and dining areas. Rocks and bricks can be turned into "rugs" to anchor these areas.

5. Bring indoor furniture out to the porch. If the space is sheltered from the weather, use wood cupboards and tables.

6. Opt for new, weather-resistant fabrics that bring a soft touch and a shot of color to outdoor spaces. Woven plastic rugs work great on porches and decks too.

7. Plant pots and urns as permanent flower arrangements you can enjoy throughout the growing season.

8. Light up the night. A few candles might be all you need. Strings of electrical lights can stretch from a building to a tree to provide diffuse lighting. Consider a chandelier to dress up a porch.

9. Play with texture. The surfaces of flowers and leaves offer plenty of opportunity. So, too, do the materials of a garden, such as brick, stone, metal, and wood.

10. Use favorite collections, such as ironstone pitchers, to hold just-picked garden flowers. Turn vintage rakes into sculpture on the side of a shed.

Live in the garden

A table and chairs turn one corner of the yard into an outdoor dining room, OPPOSITE. Stones laid underfoot and around a blanket of moss imitate the look of a rug. Planted urns serve as tabletop centerpieces.

Dress the porch

Lattice panels enclose this outdoor dining area and provide a sense of intimacy, LEFT. Folding chairs slipcovered in white turn the porch into an elegant setting for a dinner party. Three cauliflower heads march down the wood tabletop for an unexpected centerpiece.

Collect wicker pieces

Wicker furniture and cottages go together like cream and strawberries. Keep the look summery with white paint and neutral cushions, LEFT. That leaves plenty of room to inject your own style with pillows made from vintage floral fabrics.

Blend indoors and out

Weathered adult- and child-size Adirondack chairs, BELOW, look fresh and sophisticated against the pure-white paint of the buildings. By adding elements such as a fireplace to a porch, OPPOSITE, the screened space functions as any indoor room—as long as the weather is nice.

Wrap a sink in style

Plant a row

Embrace flower power

Wrap a sink in style

Putting vintage pieces to new uses works indoors and out. This kitchen sink looks perfectly at home in the garden thanks to a skirt of woven willow. The sink serves as a staging area for just-picked vegetables and flowers. A mirror above the sink [not shown] reflects the garden beyond.

Plant a row

Lined up for a flea market, these vintage metal chairs reflect the colors of the flower garden, a good source for palette inspiration. Manufactured starting in the 1940s, the chairs offer a nostalgic look back and also have modern appeal. Create your own seating area along a flower garden, or gather four chairs around a table.

Embrace flower power

Rustic yard art blooms above McCoy flowerpots, all in soft shades of blue and green. Collecting by color and shape is a smart way to build a collection that works together. Although these pieces are shown on a porch, they also would be a fun way to bring the cottage garden indoors.

COMFORT

Relaxing in style

Cottage style comes in a range of looks, but comfort is always key. Here's how to keep things relaxed.

● Select comfortable furniture, whether it's for indoors or out. An upholstered piece should have generous proportions and welcoming arms so it's as comfortable for napping as for sitting.

● Collect furniture that can take wear and tear. Paint can be a little worn so new nicks only add to the patina. If a piece is so precious that you want to protect it, it's probably not right for a cottage.

● Make sure seating pieces can be gathered close for conversation. The arrangement, rather than the pieces themselves, matters most. Group everything around an ottoman or coffee table so there's room to put up your feet or set down a glass.

● Opt for style that's not too serious. Before you buy something, think about how it fits with the way you live. It's easy to get comfortable on the porch, but cottage style is built around the idea that every room should be that relaxed and inviting.

● Choose flexible pieces that can move where you need them. Side chairs might gather by the fireplace or snuggle up to the table when company arrives.

● Add a rocking chair or two, especially on the porch. Wicker really will enhance the porch mood.

● Relax any indoor space with pieces from the garden, such as urns and glass-top patio tables.

10

cottage notebook—style ideas

Sometimes one new idea is all it takes to launch a decorating project. Short on time, but ready for a redo? Our cottage notebook is full of ideas you can start and finish in an hour, a day, or a weekend. Start simple with a single bloom in an antique glass bottle, *right*. Tea-stain fabric for cottage curtains and bed linens with vintage appeal. Advance to projects, such as slipcovers, that require more time and experience. Every project offers the opportunity to discover the artist within. Start now to bring new cottage style home.

Slipcovers with personality

Fashion magazines are the muse for slipcover designer Carrie Raphael. As she flips through their pages, she imagines how a detail from a dress—a line of buttons, a pleat, or a bow—can be used on a slipcover. In fact, she treats chairs like one-of-a-kind dressmaker's mannequins, dressing them to call attention to shapely legs or well-formed backs, RIGHT and OPPOSITE. Forget the slouchy slipcovers in fashion five years back. Raphael describes her covers as very precise, designed to closely fit chairs or sofas and with details that enhance them. One chair may have kick pleats at the corners and cording; another may feature a gathered flounce and floppy ties. Some chairs have floor-length skirts; others show a little leg. But no matter how you finish it, Raphael says, every cottage room should have one great chair with the perfect slipcover.

Condition candles in the freezer

Ring around the posies

This olive tray is ready for company, and there's not an olive in sight. Instead, lime-green button mums fill the tray in an updated version of a 1930s flower ring. It's part cottage, part modern, and totally fresh. Keep it out year-round with these seasonal favorites: spring pansies, summer roses, fall dahlias, winter pepperberry.

so they burn more slowly.

Hang a chandelier to lend a dressy note to a hardworking room, such as a kitchen or bath.

Tough-love fabric treatment

Raphael often picks up vintage curtains, bed linens, and tablecloths to pair with inexpensive fabrics, such as cotton canvas or shirting. Here's how she gives the fabrics—new and old—the soft, worn look she loves.

1. Toss the yardage in hot water for at least two washings.

2. Throw the fabrics into a hot dryer with at least 24 sheets of fabric softener.

3. Wash the pieces again to remove the film from the dryer sheets.

4. Dry the yardage without softener.

The fabric feels soft to the touch and will get softer each time you wash it. "Just like old jeans," she says. Maintain the fabrics by gently washing and drying when they're soiled.

Refurbish a flea market dresser

Two wallpaper patterns provide the style in this flea market makeover. Try this technique for any vintage piece you want to cover. Paint an old dresser with semigloss paint. Using tissue paper, make patterns of the dresser parts you want to cover with wallpaper. Lay the patterns on the wallpaper, taking care to center and match the wallpaper design. Cut out the pieces. Spread wallpaper-border adhesive on the wallpaper back, following label instructions. Adhere wallpaper to the furniture; smooth.

Make a statement on a sofa with two big pillows rather than a lot of little pillows.

Writing in the sand

Glass plates provide the clear view you'll need to create this summertime table setting. Spoon a few tablespoons of sand in the center of a white plate, and gently spread the sand to cover a circle. Using your finger, draw the initial of a guest's name in the sand, then top it off with a clear glass plate. Repeat for each guest. No need for place cards.

Keeping tabs

Metal pegs, door hooks, and vintage nails might seem unlikely curtain hardware, but lined up across window molding, they lend a casual look even to elegant fabrics. Just make the curtains with tab tops or ribbon ties to hang from the hardware.

Castoff comebacks

Adopt a flea market find and give it a new job. This 1940s utility cart, revamped into a movable bar, looks ready for service once more. Try these other projects: Cluster three metal swivel stools in place of a coffee table, use a faucet handle as a towel hook, or turn a metal washtub into a water garden.

Chalk it up

Plain closet doors have a modern-cottage attitude thanks to paint that's perfect for chalk. To make your blackboard, mark off the area using painter's tape, then apply four coats of chalkboard paint with a foam roller. Or remove the doors, lay them flat, and spray them with chalkboard paint. Wait three hours and write away.

Anyone for tea?

Brand-new fabrics absorb vintage appeal when you soak them in a tea bath. The final effect is subtly uneven tones. Start with 100 percent cotton, linen, silk, or wool fabric. Wash to remove sizing and surface chemicals; don't use fabric softener. Dye using these steps.

1. Bundle 1 cup of loose tea leaves in cheesecloth (one bundle per 6 cups of water).

2. Place the bundles in a pot of water; bring to a boil. Let water cool. Remove bundles.

3. Soak fabrics directly in the pot, adding ½ cup vinegar during the last five minutes of the tea bath. Vinegar helps set the stain.

4. When the desired color is achieved, rinse the fabric under running water. Hang to dry.

NOTE: Experiment with different types of tea, concentrations of tea, and soaking times. After staining fabric, rinse it once and dry to see the color. If it's not what you envisioned, return the fabric to the pot.

Add sparkle to a pillow by attaching an antique rhinestone pin to the corner.

Top it off

Slipcovers work their magic updating chairs and sofas. But the bedside table? This simple ticking stripe, treated to welted edges and a flouncy skirt, transforms a small table. Consider covering a coffee table or dining table as well. The fitted style and dressmaker details of a slipcover make it much more than a tablecloth. And just like every slipcover, it's easy to slip off and into the wash.

real shiners

Flea market lamps offer an inexpensive canvas for your creative efforts. One lamp is great, but a matching pair is even better. To start, rip out the old wiring and take the lamps to your local lighting store, where it will cost about $20 per lamp to have them rewired. Prime, then paint the bases. Protect the finish with a coat of protective clear enamel sealer. Select your new shades and add an elegant detail of bead trim glued around the bottom. Crystal finials from a lighting store add a sparkling finish.

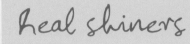

To make filmy curtains stand out like a ball gown, line them with tulle.

Bold-plated

Three trim pieces meant for the top of a door turn a blank wall into a dapper doorless cupboard. Look for old headers at architectural salvage stores and new ones at home centers. Attach a thin strip of screen molding to the top edge of each to keep plates from slipping. Paint the shelves with primer and two coats of enamel. Screw the plate shelves to the wall, leaving 12 inches between them.

Shell seeking

Buy the ingredients for these projects from an online source, such as www.seashellcity.com, www.seashells.com, or www.shellsaplenty.com.

SHELL PULLS: Glue shells onto drawer handles using two-part epoxy. Or drill through each shell, starting with a small drill bit and gradually increasing the size of the bit until you make a hole big enough for a screw. Screw the shells to the drawer.

SHELL SWAG: Create this simple swag with pearls, shells, and sand dollars. Top each shell with a bell cap from the crafts store; glue it in place with epoxy. Tie the shells and sand dollars to a pearl strand using ribbon; secure with hot glue. Swag the shell-filled pearls within a window frame; add a second, unadorned pearl swag.

SHELL CABINET: Photocopy pages of a vintage book and adhere them to a display cabinet with decoupage medium. Use the shelves as simple display spaces for your favorite shells.

Go with the glow

There's more than candlelight giving these simple votives some shimmer. Silver leaf bought in sheets at the crafts store is the secret. Here's how it's done.

1. Wash glass votive in soapy water, then rinse in a 10:1 water/vinegar solution.

2. Coat the interior of the votives with spray adhesive. Allow it to dry until it's clear and tacky.

3. Transfer the silver leaf using the tissue sheets packed between the sheets of silver leaf. Rub the leaf onto the tacky surface, then remove the tissue. After coating the surface, rub it with a cotton ball to remove any excess silver leaf.

4. Seal the surface with a coat or two of clear acrylic sealer.

If you can't find lampshades in the perfect color, spray-paint them. That goes for the fabric ones too.

Holding power

Invented to hold up a beam or stand sentinel at a doorway, new or antique corbels can be put to less strenuous use. Here's how.

○ Place a corbel, top down, on a dresser and prop a framed print on it.

○ Use a row of corbels to display favorite plates along a dining room wall. Stick a tack into the top of each corbel to keep the plates from slipping away.

○ Attach corbels at the top corners of a window. Orient the corbel so its curves will hold a bamboo curtain rod.

○ Set one corbel on the floor as a doorstop.

The hang of it

Give botanical prints the attention they deserve with matching frames. Hang them from lengths of string, wire, or cable looped over vintage nails, cup hooks, screw hooks, decorative hooks, cabinet handles, or curtain pins. It's a modern way to show off your cottage favorites.

Index